FATTY LIVER DIET COOKBOOK

1500-Day Easy and Mouthwatering Recipes to Detox and Cleanse your Liver. Live Healthier without Sacrificing Taste. Includes 30-Day Meal Plan

Melissa Jordon

ISBN: 979-8351130750
10 9 8 7 6 5 4 3 2 1

MELISSA JORDON
collection

DOWNLOAD YOUR GIFT NOW!

The bonus is **100% FREE.**
You don't need to enter any details except your name and email address.

To download your bonus scan the QR code below or go to

https://melissajordon.me/bonus-fl/

SCAN ME

ANTI-INFLAMMATORY
Cookbook
for Beginners

1200 Day Recipes to Improve
Your Health, Reduce
Inflammation and Lose Weight

Table of Contents

Introduction

Dietary fats have a significant role in overall health. Essential fatty acids like linoleic acid are found in these fats, providing energy and supporting a healthy metabolism. Non-alcoholic fatty liver disease (NAFLD) may be linked to a person's intake of harmful fats, according to recent studies. As the name indicates, Fatty liver disease is a medical condition in which fat accumulates in the liver.

Two types exist; those caused by excessive alcohol consumption and those that aren't caused by alcohol use. In the United States, alcoholic fatty liver disease affects around 5% of the population.

Abdominal swelling, high heart rate, and extra weight around the waist indicate fatty liver. Foods high in vitamin B6 and polyunsaturated fats make up the bulk of the fatty liver diet. A low-carbohydrate diet might assist in minimizing the risk factors for non-alcoholic fatty liver disease, such as elevated cholesterol levels or triglyceride levels in the blood serum.

Patients with non-alcoholic fatty liver disease are becoming more prevalent, yet the cause of their condition remains a mystery.

Metabolic syndrome, a group of conditions that includes insulin resistance, dyslipidemia, and increases in body mass index (BMI), maybe the primary cause of liver fat buildup.

Diets high in unsaturated fatty acids have increased the risk of non-alcoholic fatty liver disease because of the high-fat content (90 percent). The lack of sufficient randomized trials makes it impossible for researchers to determine whether the link between the two is causal or results from confounding variables.

According to the American Liver Foundation, there are no medical treatments for non-alcoholic fatty liver disease. Eating a healthy diet and exercising regularly are the best ways to avoid liver damage and treat it when it has already occurred. No matter what kind of liver illness you have, the best treatment is to make lifestyle changes, including losing weight, abstaining from alcohol, and eating food low in saturated fat.

Signs and Symptoms:

Many patients with Fatty Liver Disease are usually asymptomatic, with the liver often discovered by 'mistake' perhaps during liver enzymes examination in the laboratory. Apart from hepatitis (inflammation of the liver) and other chronic liver diseases, Fatty Liver Disease is the most common reason for the unexplained rise in the liver enzyme levels during various laboratory investigations.

The most common features that suggest fatty liver disease after the persistent increase in liver enzymes are:

- Fatigue/general body weakness
- Discoloration of the skin
- Unexplained weight loss
- Nausea
- Abdominal discomfort, especially in the right upper quadrant
- Hepatomegaly (Enlargement of the liver)

There could be liver cirrhosis (scarring of the liver) which reveals the progression of the disease. There are also complaints of pruritis (Intense itching) and jaundice, including portal hypertension. Many of the patients equally possess metabolic syndrome-associated features such as Diabetes mellitus (Fasting blood glucose > 110mg/dl), obesity (BMI > 30kg/m), hypertension (Blood Pressure > 130/85 mmHg), and Hyperlipidemia (Blood Lipid Level >250mg/dl).

Diagnosis:

This disease can be incidentally diagnosed via the persistent elevation of liver enzymes or when monitoring for some side effects of specific medication especially cholesterol-lowering drugs, or even when checking for some non-specific symptoms in the body. It can also be detected less often after imaging or liver biopsy that was done for other investigations.

However, the disease diagnosis can be made using the primary non-invasive evaluation which is better than the liver biopsy examination (which has a higher risk and it's not cost-effective). Routine laboratory evaluation of liver enzymes and clinical factors investigations, especially among patients who are obese, diabetic or whose liver enzymes are persistently elevated, has proven to reveal more severe fatty disease which can help make other decisions about when to order a liver biopsy examination.

Causes of Fatty Liver Disease

Excess fat is accumulated in liver cells and adds to fatty liver disease. Several circumstances can cause this fat accumulation. AFLD may be caused by excessive alcohol consumption.

Heavy drinking may cause fluctuations in the liver's metabolic systems. Some of the metabolic products may react with fatty acids, creating fats that can build up in the liver.

The etiology of fatty liver disease in those who don't consume much alcohol is less understood. It's conceivable that these people's bodies create too much fat or don't digest fat effectively enough.

One or more of the following variables may have a role in the development of fatty liver disease in persons who don't drink much alcohol:

- Obesity
- Type 2 diabetes
- Insulin resistance
- Elevated blood fat levels, particularly triglycerides
- Metabolic syndrome

Other factors contributing to the fatty liver include pregnancy; pharmaceutical adverse effects; infections, hepatitis C, and some uncommon hereditary diseases.

Risk Factors of Fatty Liver Disease

To detect fatty liver, it is essential to identify the risk factors that may trigger the onset of this disease. Alcoholism is a primary risk factor for alcoholic fatty liver disease. Men who consume more than four pints or eight units of alcohol and women who drink five units daily are more likely to develop this disorder.

In addition to alcohol consumption, several other important factors can also lead to the development of the fatty liver.

Lifestyle

"Studies have proven that sitting for only 2 hours right after a meal can reduce insulin sensitivity and increase the levels of blood sugar, predisposing to fatty liver."

Lifestyle is said to accelerate the development of fatty liver significantly. Overeating, paired with a sedentary life, primarily contributes to the progression of this disease.

Insulin resistance is commonly observed as a side effect of eating too much and not exercising. It is also one of the main reasons fats accumulate in the liver. Within the body, insulin resistance initiates the release of fatty acids from the fat cells, and sugar develops in the blood. The excessive amount of sugar and fatty acids from the diet and blood make their way to the liver and are converted to fat and then stored in the hepatocytes.

As long as the muscles, liver, and adipose cells remain resistant to insulin, sugar loading in the blood and fat accumulation in the liver will continue. This turns into a vicious cycle that keeps repeating itself to exacerbate the state of the fatty liver.

Eating a lot of sugar and fat allows the cell to fill up with energy. At some point, the energy level becomes so high that the cells fail to respond to insulin. Under such circumstances, the liver has to receive all excessive sugars and fats and store them in its cells to save the body from the destructive impacts of high levels of sugar and fat in the blood.

The fastest way in which you can increase the fat build-up is by eating too many carbohydrates. Fructose, in particular, causes fat accumulation in the liver. This is important since the control of fatty liver through diet rests around this concept.

Observing a sedentary lifestyle can also make your body cells respond less to insulin. Imagine what will happen to your body if you keep sitting most of the time while most of the meals you consume are overloaded with fats and carbohydrates.

This is the reason why the majority of the researchers agree upon the fact that improvement of insulin sensitivity can essentially treat fatty liver disease.

Genetics

Like a lot of other diseases, fatty liver disease is polygenic. This means that specific genes and their interactions can increase or decrease a person's susceptibility to the development of the fatty liver.

One of the genetic variants is of particular importance in this regard. The variant is known as PNPLA3 I148M and is highly associated with the development of the fatty liver. This does not even require the presence of other problems such as insulin resistance, dyslipidemia, diabetes, or even obesity.

However, this does not mean that the presence of genes means you will suffer from this disease. For instance, the PNPLA3 I148M gene variant can cause the progression of the disease only in the combination of other factors such as unhealthy dietary patterns, alcohol abuse, inactivity, viral infection, and a high amount of fructose.

The fact that fatty liver disease is polygenic justifies why fatty liver disease tends to exist in clusters within different families. This is why adopting an extremely healthy lifestyle is essential if your ancestors have been struggling with this disease.

Other genetic factors may also impact your likelihood of developing this disease. These factors may include ethnicity and gender, affecting the chance of developing fatty liver disease. Some older studies have also found that women are naturally more susceptible to developing this disease, but now it is being said that it is more commonly seen in men.

Scientists have also postulated that the gender difference in fatty liver is possibly due to the difference in fat distribution and the concentration of hormones. Men are fatter stored close to their organs which is the type of fat that is inflammatory. This pattern of fat deposition increases the risk of fatty liver and many other diseases in males. On the other hand, women are more likely to accumulate fat in the thighs and hips which is less inflammatory than males.

As far as ethnicity is concerned, studies have established that African Americans are exposed to the lowest risk of developing fatty liver despite being highly exposed to the risk of developing type 2 diabetes. This difference is justified because of the different patterns of fat deposition too. In contrast, Hispanics and Asians seem to have the most significant risk of fatty liver disease. Scientists believe this is because these two ethnicities are more likely to store their fat in close proximity to organs.

It is essential to mention that other genes might also have specific effects on the development of the fatty liver. These might not be your genes but the genes in your microbiome.

Gut Health Issues

Your microbiome consists of over 100 trillion bacteria, usually lining your gut. These different types of bacteria that keep flourishing and perishing from time to time have an essential effect on your health, especially on the health of the liver.

Scientific studies focusing on the microbiome of different obese patients have established that such patients have a reduced amount of a particular type of bacteria. This specific bacterium is known as Bacteroidetes. At the same time, the levels of another bacteria known as Firmicutes are increased. This disturbance in the ratio of these two species of bacteria causes an increase in the absorption of lipopolysaccharides.

What are these lipopolysaccharides? These components are found in the cell membranes of most gram-negative bacterial species, such as Bacteroidetes. However, these components are not harmful. Lipopolysaccharides are, in fact, endotoxins that stimulate a robust inflammatory response within the body. This helps to contribute to the development of insulin resistance in the liver and leads to obesity.

The microbiome of every person is unique. However, it has become quite clear about the source which generates this obesity-inducing microbiome. The source is a diet that causes the development of obesity, more specifically, a diet rich in sugar and fat. Consuming a diet high in fat and sugar causes a reduction in the microbiome diversity and disturbs the Firmicutes-to-Bacteroidetes ratio. This will result in the development of obesity-causing microbiome profiles that favors the progression of fatty liver disease.

Moreover, the increase in the absorption of lipopolysaccharide due to the consumption of a poor diet and an obesity-causing microbiota can disturb the liver functions so much that fatty acids may even progress to steatohepatitis.

Miscellaneous Causes

Various hereditary problems like hemochromatosis, Wilson's disease, Alagille syndrome, galactosemia, type 1 storage disease, and alpha-1 antitrypsin deficiency can naturally predispose a person to a higher risk of developing fatty liver.

People already suffering from some kind of autoimmune disorder are also susceptible to developing fatty liver disease. In such cases, the liver is already targeted for damage by the immune system, and the development of fatty liver only worsens things. In addition, disorders of the bile duct, including primary sclerosing cholangitis and primary biliary cirrhosis, may also contribute to fatty liver.

In some cases, inhalation or ingesting toxins can also precipitate fatty liver. The significance of toxic hepatitis is worth mentioning in this regard. Certain drugs, including prescription and over-the-counter medications, can sometimes lead to severe reactions, consequently developing fatty liver. People already infected with viruses, such as hepatitis A, B, or C virus, are more likely to develop fatty liver.

How To Prevent a Fatty Liver Disease

Pay attention to the nutritional information

Make a habit of checking processed foods' nutritional information when shopping, especially sugar content. You may be surprised at how many products contain high levels of sugar, even ones you wouldn't have guessed. In general, this is not about banning yourself from everything that contains sugar because, let's face it, you don't last long. Therefore, it makes more sense to first develop an awareness of the amount of sugar in the foods you eat frequently.

Fresh ingredients instead of ready meals

Especially with many ready meals, one often does not expect the high sugar content because they usually do not taste sweet. One way to avoid unknown sources of sugar is to cook with fresh ingredients instead of relying on ready-made meals. This book, with its numerous liver-friendly recipes, will show you that this does not necessarily require much effort and that there are multiple ways of putting it into practice simply.

In general, that doesn't mean that you can never enjoy your favorite frozen pizza again. It should be the exception rather than the rule in your otherwise fresh-ingredient diet.

Mix yoghurt yourself

Most types of yoghurt in the refrigerated section contain a lot of sugar. An easy way to avoid this is to buy a jar of natural yoghurt and mix it yourself with berries, for example. Not only are frozen berries usually cheaper, but they also produce juice when they are thawed, which is excellent for yoghurt. Even if you now add some sugar because the berries are otherwise too sour for you, you can control the amount yourself, unlike with ready-made yoghurt.

Write yourself a shopping list

That sounds banal, but it can make a big difference. This will make you more aware of your usual shopping habits, and since you now pay more attention to the sugar content of your food, you can plan your purchase more specifically with the help of such a note. Very few people succeed in radically changing their diet immediately and permanently, which is not even necessary. Instead, gradually replace the products with the highest sugar and fat content in your purchase with healthier alternatives. For example, if you used to buy five ready-to-eat meals for a week, now buy only two and replace the other three with freshly prepared meals. That way, with recurring successes to be proud of, it's much easier to build long-term motivation and gradually increase the amount of fresh food in your diet.

Three solid meals a day

Eat three solid meals a day. The liver and the body must be given enough time to recover after each meal. This is where the five-hour rule comes in handy. It states that at least five hours should elapse after each meal before the next one. The easiest way to ensure this is with fixed meal times. For example, if you have breakfast at 8 a.m., lunch at 1 p.m., and dinner at 6 p.m., there are five hours between each meal. Of course, not everyone has the luxury of being utterly free regarding mealtimes. But even in professional life and shift work, it can be possible to stick to this simple rule by approaching at least about five hours without eating after each meal, thus making it a habit.

In general, larger snacks between meals are not recommended. Still, like everything else, this rule should not be exaggerated if you want to implement it with motivation in the long term. If you stick to the five-hour rule 5 out of 7 days a week and completely avoid snacking in between, that's an achievement you can be proud of and will do your well-being and your liver good.

Drink enough

Some of the body's daily liquid comes from food, but that's not enough. It is essential to ensure that you drink at least 1.5 liters a day. How much we consume (and what, see point 7) is vital for detoxifying the body because everything you ingest ends up in the liver. Sufficient fluid intake ensures that toxins in the body can be transported to the liver more quickly and broken down there. Simply put, staying hydrated helps your liver work and contributes to your overall well-being. If you find it challenging to drink enough, it can help to buy mineral water in small 0.5-liter bottles. In these, the amount of liquid subjectively often looks less than it is. If you now plan to empty three such bottles a day, you might reach the goal of 1.5 liters a day more easily. It can also help to schedule these three bottles throughout the day, for example, one after getting up until 12 p.m., one until 4 p.m. and one until 8 p.m. Of course, this does not mean you are only allowed to drink mineral water.

If this tip helps you, you can also fill other suitable drinks into half-liter bottles like this. We will now determine which drinks are generally appropriate and which are not.

Drinking is not just drinking

Watch what you drink. Soft drinks, in particular, usually contain vast amounts of sugar and the light or zero variants are only recommended to a limited extent. Some studies suggest artificial sweeteners increase the risk of cardiovascular disease. Here, however, the opinions of the experts often differ widely.

What is certain, however, is that it is best for you when bottled water makes up a high percentage of your daily fluid intake. Tea is also very suitable for various varieties of low-calorie and low-sugar drinks. Of course, there is also nothing wrong with one or two cups of coffee a day, preferably without sugar.

Fruit juices naturally contain a lot of sugar but are recommended in a mixing ratio of 1:4 with mineral water, i.e., as a diluted spritzer. Another way to spice up water is to add lemon slices or peppermint leaves. Even homemade smoothies can bring variety. In general, homemade smoothies are far better than store-bought ready-made versions, as they often contain a lot of sugar. A little work on your mixer will also save you money in the long run.

Get enough exercise

In addition to numerous other positive effects, regular exercise can be beneficial and valuable for fatty liver. Physical exertion positively impacts the metabolism, among other things, which means that fat can be broken down in the liver.

It is always essential that the type of movement you choose suits you and is fun to a certain extent. That's why everything that has to do with movement makes sense and is suitable, whereby the consistent basic rule is more valuable than intensive. An hour's daily walk is much better than doing a few vigorous workouts and then quickly cutting it out altogether.

There are also no limits to the imagination here. One prefers to go for a walk, the next rides a bike and the third likes to work out on the home trainer. It is essential to take it slow and create a workload that you can realistically keep up with for a long time or gradually increase. Discussing your plans with your family doctor makes sense if you decide to do sports.

The topic of losing weight

One often hears, also in connection with fatty liver, that losing weight is very important. Indeed, this is not wrong, especially if you are overweight. However, time is an important point here because "reduce over time" absolutely excludes radical diets. A rapid weight reduction, as is promised in practically every second magazine, can even have a counterproductive effect in the case of a fatty liver and make the fatty liver even worse. You should not lose more than half a kilo to a maximum of one kilo per week.

If you are overweight, you can achieve this automatically with a balanced and healthy diet and without any miracle diet. Eating healthy doesn't mean you have to give up sweets entirely. In the long run, it makes much more sense to eat something sweet consciously and carefully than to ban it overnight completely. For example, treat yourself to a candy bar to reward yourself for something you've accomplished rather than casually eating it. A pleasant side effect is that the pleasure you eat sweet increases enormously.

Watch your stress level

Avoid stress as much as possible. If you often suffer from a stressful everyday life, it harms your liver. When stressed, your liver produces more blood sugar, which can reduce blood sugar levels. In addition, stress also harms the blood flow to the liver and digestive tract, further reducing their ability to perform their functions. That being said, stress has a few other adverse effects on your body. Of course, very few people enjoy a completely stress-free everyday life; to a particular extent, stress can also trigger positive outcomes, such as higher performance.

On the other hand, some ways to deal with permanent and unhealthy stress are better. This includes the movement described, which can usually help "let off steam" quite quickly. Of course, a healthy diet also makes a significant contribution. In addition, you should allow yourself breaks when you need them, even if it's sometimes just a few minutes to take a deep breath. Meditation or special breathing techniques are also stressed killers that don't cost much but can bring you a lot. You will find numerous free and beneficial written instructions or videos on the Internet under the keywords "meditation" or "breathing techniques for relaxation." The general rule here is: Don't try everything at once! Only do what is good for you and integrate it as much as possible into your everyday life.

The Perfect Diet for Fatty Liver Disease

Healthy diet consumption implies striking a good balance between various foods. For most people, it means consuming more vegetables, fruits, high-fiber, starchy diets with little or no fats (incredibly saturated), salt, and sugar.

At this juncture, I will give you a Nine-step approach to healthy diet consumption. Relax, read and assimilate it into your bloodstream and make it part of your daily activity.

Consume Regular Meals:

Select your meal carefully and ensure breakfast, lunch, and supper daily. Don't skip meals for any reason unless you have healthy fasting. Regularly eating allows you to control your appetite and how hungry you feel, which has the advantage of preventing you from eating unsolicited and junk foods at intervals. You can likewise have other benefits such as control of your blood sugar and lipid (fat) level.

Reduce Your Fat Consumption:

Try as much as possible to reduce the rate you consume fats, particularly saturated fats because they increase your blood cholesterol levels. Fat has a very high-calorie content meaning that you can lose that weight when you cut out or cut down the rate at which you consume them. You can choose to consume unsaturated fats, especially mono-saturated fats such as olive oil and rapeseed oil.

One may then ask: *How can I cut down the quantity of fat in my diet?*

- Consume less saturated fat such as butter, full cream dairy, margarine, and lard.
- Try to use olive or rapeseed oil in your diet rather than saturated oils, which cause health hazards. However, "moderation is the key" when using olive and rapeseed oil as they contain some calories.
- Eat more fish, turkey, lean chicken, lentils, and beans instead of eating fatty meat (e.g., Lamb), sausages, and pies. Ensure that your diets contain oily fish at least twice per week.
- Avoid eating processed or over-processed foods (e.g., Pizza), takeaways, or junk because they contain high fat and salt content. However, if you cannot do without eating processed foods, then choose the low fats instead.
- Avoid high-fat snacks (e.g., biscuits, cakes, doughnuts, nuts, and crips). However, the nut contains some healthy oils so you may choose to eat them but not frequently.
- Ensure to cook rather than frying; you can prefer to boil, bake, grill or steam your meals. They are best options than frying. You can trim those fats off the meat or take off the skin of your

chicken. If your casseroles and soup contain fats, then remove those fats by skimming the surface of the soup.

Equip your food with starchy carbohydrates:

Starchy foods are always a good source of energy, and most contain nutrients that are bread, noodles, potatoes, pasta, rice, and yam, among many others. However, ensure that you consume whole grain carbohydrates or those rich in fiber than refined or white carbohydrates, which will complicate the disease.

Carbohydrates digest slowly and make you less hungry because you will feel fuller for a long time, enabling you to consume less food. Your digestive system will be healthy as problems such as constipation will be avoided.

Most fiber-rich carbohydrates have a low glycemic index (GI), meaning they are absorbed slowly and possess the ability to control blood glucose levels. This is important, especially among diabetic patients, as non-diabetics are equally advantaged if they adopt this starchy food consumption approach.

Some examples of starchy grains you are advised to eat are:

- Bread (e.g., Pumpernickel, granary and rye).
- Cereals- (e.g., Bran flakes, natural muesli and oats porridge).
- Rice- Brown rice, basmati and wholegrain.

Consume More fruits and Vegetables:

Fruits and vegetables contain enough minerals, vitamins and fibers for your health and fitness. They also can prevent many sorts of cancer and with their low-calorie content they can help you lose that extra weight. Therefore, ensure that your diet contains at least four (4) portions. Check out the keto diet guide on the subsequent pages.

Consume More Lentils and Beans:

These (chickpeas, butter peas, green and red lentils, etc.) do not affect your blood glucose levels, unlike many other foods. Therefore, they play good roles in controlling your blood cholesterol levels. Add them to your soups, stews, salads, casseroles, etc.

Consume At Least 3 portions of Oily Fish /week:

Oily fish contains polyunsaturated fats called omega-3, which help to guide your heart from diseases and also help to minimize high levels of blood lipids. Thus, it can stop your fatty liver from being worse. Examples of some oily fishes include:

- Sardines
- Herrings
- Kippers
- Mackerel
- Salmon
- Trout
- Fresh tuna
- Pilchards

So, when next you go for your shopping, try to have one or more of these fish in your cart, okay?

Eat less sugary drinks and food:

A more recommended alternative for sugary drinks is to drink squashes. If you must take fruit juice, ensure that it's not more than 200ml/day as it contains high sugar. For diabetic patients, it is not recommended to consume diabetic food as it can be sweetened with fructose and sorbitol, which almost contain fats and can complicate the situation (check out the diet regimen in subsequent pages). They also possess a laxative effect and can be expensive.

Control Your Alcohol Consumption:

Although this type of Fatty Liver Disease we are dealing with is not caused by alcohol, the condition can be worsened by alcohol consumption. Therefore, it is a wonderful idea to cut down or stop the consumption of alcohol altogether. Do you know that alcohol contains a lot of calories? Thus, reducing your consumption rate will help you lose that excess weight.

Alcohol is measured in units written on the bottle, can, or box that reveals the quantity of alcohol in a liter. For example, 5% implies that there are 5 units in a liter. Thus, if you consume 500ml of beer, you must have taken 2.5 units of alcohol.

Unit Recommendations according to World Health Organization (WHO)

- Men should take no more than 20 units of alcohol in a week and not more than 4 units per day.
- Women should take units not more than 14 per week and not more than 3 per day.

You may be wondering how to calculate the units of alcohol in a drink. Okay, I got your back.

Let's do a little mathematics. (You can calculate this by multiplying the unit by the size of your drink and then dividing by 1000ml).

For instance, a standard 500ml of beer with 5% alcohol can be calculated thus;

$$500 \times 5 = 2500; \text{ then divide by } 1000ml = 2.5 \text{ units}$$

Hope you now got the gist. It's straightforward.

Cut Down your Salt Consumption Rate:

High salt in your diet (i.e.,> 6g/day) can elevate your blood pressure. Elevated blood pressure tends to cause stroke and heart disease, leading to Fatty Liver Disease.

How, then, can you cut down your excessive salt consumption?

- Run away from processed and junk foods as quickly as your feet can carry you.
- Do not put extra salt in your meal while eating; always do such while cooking the food.
- You can decide to use spices and herbs to bring out the flavor of your food, which prevents you from adding extra salt to improve the food taste.

Alright, we are done with the Nine Step Approach that will help you prevent or improve the status of your fatty liver disease. When you stick to these methods we have discussed, there is no doubt that your body will be renewed for the better within a month.

CHAPTER 1: Types of Fatty Liver Disease

Nonalcoholic Fatty Liver Disease (NAFLD)

As the name suggests, non-alcoholic fatty liver disease is a condition with a fat buildup in the liver cells, even if the patient does not drink alcohol excessively. In the initial stages, the fat deposits may not trigger any symptoms. Still, it has been found that in some cases, this may progress to inflammation called Nonalcoholic Steatohepatitis (NASH), which further can lead to scarring of the tissues in the liver and even cirrhosis.

People may still develop a fatty liver without excessive consumption of alcohol. There could be several factors or reasons for developing a fatty liver. Your likelihood of developing fatty liver conditions is higher if:

- Have diabetes.
- Are obese or overweight
- An insulin resistance body where your body does not respond to insulin as it should.
- Have high blood cholesterol.

You may be advised to change your diet and lifestyle if you have been diagnosed with non-alcoholic fatty liver disease. These diet and lifestyle changes include:

- Eating a lot of vegetables and fruits.
- Eating slow-release starchy foods, such as potatoes and bread.
- Doing regular exercises such as walking, jogging or swimming.
- Reduce or stop the consumption of alcohol.
- Avoid refined sugars and saturated fats in chocolate, cakes, and biscuits.

Maintaining a healthy weight for your age and build is also recommended. If you have diabetes, it is suggested to work with your doctor to keep your blood sugar levels under reasonable control. Consult your doctor if you have issues with high blood cholesterol levels or are insulin resistant.

Alcoholic Fatty Liver Disease (AFLD)

If you are a heavy drinker or have been drinking alcohol excessively, this is the first stage of injury to your liver due to the buildup of fatty deposits. If proper care is taken and you stay away from alcohol, this can be reversed entirely. As per the studies, only 20% of people with alcohol-related fatty liver develop inflammation (alcoholic hepatitis) and eventually cirrhosis.

People who have been drinking alcohol excessively and have alcoholic liver damage have been found primarily malnourished or underweight, which means their body lacks the nutrients required to function properly. This lack of nourishment could be due to several factors. Some common ones are:

- If you are not eating well and just drinking, you ask your body to work hard to process alcohol. Alcohol has no nutritional value but requires a lot of energy for the body to process.
- Poor or unbalanced diet.
- Loss of appetite due to heavy drinking. If you drink and smoke, the condition will worsen. Smoking is known for suppressing hunger.
- Poor absorption of food nutrients as the liver is less able to produce bile to aid digestion.

You could be undernourished even if you are overweight. It all depends on what and how you eat. If you eat well and still becoming overweight, get yourself checked, if not already. This condition could be due to fluid retention.

You should be prescribed vitamin B if you have been drinking excessively or at harmful levels. People with the alcoholic liver disease generally lack the vitamin called thiamin, a vitamin B that helps the body convert carbohydrates into energy. Consult your doctor or dietitian if this has not been prescribed.

Acute Fatty Liver of Pregnancy (AFLP)

This fatty liver disease occurs when excess fat builds up in the liver during pregnancy. It's a rare but severe pregnancy complication. The exact cause is unknown, while genetics may be a reason.

When the acute fatty liver of pregnancy develops, it usually appears in the third trimester. It poses serious health risks to the mother and baby If left untreated.

If you are diagnosed with AFLP, the doctor will want to deliver your baby as soon as possible. You might need to receive follow-up care several days after giving birth.

Your liver health will likely return to normal within a few weeks of giving birth.

CHAPTER 2: Foods That Cleanse the Liver

You need to know about the benefits of certain foods so that you might be able to incorporate them into your daily diet.

Cruciferous Vegetables

These vegetables have a high level of mineral sulfur, enhancing liver detoxification. Cruciferous vegetables include Brussels sprouts, broccoli, cabbage, broccolini, and cauliflower.

Leafy Greens

Dark, leafy green vegetables have high levels of chlorophyll and vitamin K, both essential for general health. Leafy green vegetables include bok choy, mustard greens, spinach, watercress, silver beet, choy sum, and other Asian greens.

Bitter Greens

Bitter greens such as endive, radicchio, rocket, and chicory enhance bile flow.

Yoghurt

Yoghurt consists of certain friendly bacteria. Be sure to use plain, full-fat yoghurt with no sweetener, or try Greek-style yoghurt.

Omega-3 Fatty Acid-Rich Foods

Omega-3 fatty acids are required for the maintenance of healthy cell membranes. They can also decrease the inflammation of the liver cells often seen in the fatty liver. Omega-3 fatty acids can be found in sardines, salmon, tuna, mackerel, trout, hemp, flaxseeds, chia seeds, walnuts, and grass-fed lambs.

Foods with Vitamin C

Vitamin C mainly improves the function of the liver. The best sources of this vitamin are limes, lemons, oranges, grapefruits, kiwi fruit, mandarins, berries, tomatoes, and capsicum.

Onions and Garlic

Both onion and garlic consist of certain cleansing products that purify the liver and blood. It should ideally be eaten regularly. The raw form is preferable but can be used in the cooked form.

Hummus and Tahini

Tahini and hummus are both rich sources of minerals, calcium in particular. They also have high amounts of healthy fats.

Olives

Both olives, i.e. green and black, contain antioxidants and healthy fats.

Walnuts

Walnuts have high amounts of amino acid arginine and help the liver detoxify ammonia. Walnuts are also known to aid glutathione production in the liver.

Turmeric

Turmeric is also known to help boost liver detox by assisting the enzymes

Eggs

Eggs have a good amount of sulfur and protein. They are healthy for the liver and will not affect cholesterol levels. Eggs are beneficial if you are trying to lose weight and reverse fatty liver.

Avocados

Avocados have high levels of vitamin E as compared to other food items. They are incredibly healthy for liver health.

CHAPTER 3: Breakfast Recipes

1. Egg and Veggie Muffins

Preparation Time: 15 minutes
Cooking Time: 20 minutes
Servings: 4
Ingredients:

- Cooking spray
- Eggs – 4
- Unsweetened rice milk – 2 Tablespoon
- Sweet onion – ½ chopped
- Red bell pepper – ½ chopped
- Pinch red pepper flakes
- Pinch ground black pepper

Directions:

1. Preheat the oven to 350F.
2. Spray 4 muffin pans with cooking spray. Set aside.
3. Mix the milk, eggs, onion, red pepper, parsley, red pepper flakes, and black pepper until mixed.
4. Pour the egg mixture into prepared muffin pans.
5. Bake until the muffins are puffed and golden, about 18 to 20 minutes.
6. serve

Per serving: Calories: 84Kcal; Fat: 5g; Carbohydrates: 3g; Protein: 7g

2. Apple Pumpkin Muffins

Preparation Time: 15 minutes
Cooking Time: 20 minutes
Servings: 12
Ingredients:

- 1 cup all-purpose flour
- 1 cup wheat bran
- 2 teaspoons Phosphorus Powder
- 1 cup pumpkin purée
- ¼ cup honey
- ¼ cup olive oil
- 1 egg
- 1 teaspoon vanilla extract
- ½ cup cored diced apple

Directions:

1. Preheat the oven to 400°F.
2. Line 12 muffin cups with paper liners.
3. Stir together the flour, wheat bran, and baking powder, and mix this in a medium bowl.
4. Whisk together the pumpkin, honey, olive oil, egg, and vanilla in a small bowl.
5. Stir the pumpkin mixture into the flour mixture until just combined.
6. Stir in the diced apple.
7. Spoon the batter into the muffin cups.
8. Bake for about 20 minutes, or until a toothpick inserted in the center of a muffin comes out clean.

Per serving: Calories: 125Kcal; Fat: 5g; Carbohydrates: 20g; Protein: 2g

3. Spiced French Toast

Preparation Time: 15 minutes
Cooking Time: 12 minutes
Servings: 4
Ingredients:

- 4 eggs
- ½ cup Homemade Rice Milk (here, or use unsweetened store-bought) or almond milk
- ¼ cup freshly squeezed orange juice
- 1 teaspoon ground cinnamon
- ½ teaspoon ground ginger

- Pinch ground cloves
- 1 tablespoon ghee, divided
- 8 slices of white bread

Directions:

1. Whisk eggs, rice milk, orange juice, cinnamon, ginger, and cloves until well blended in a large bowl.
2. Melt half the ghee in a large skillet. It should be in medium-high heat only.
3. Dredge four of the bread slices in the egg mixture until well soaked, and place them in the skillet.
4. Cook the toast until golden brown on both sides, turning once, about 6 minutes total.
5. Repeat with the remaining ghee and bread.
6. Serve 2 pieces of hot French toast to each person.

Per serving: Calories: 236Kcal; Fat: 11g; Carbohydrates: 27g; Protein: 11g

4. Breakfast Tacos

Preparation Time: 10 minutes
Cooking Time: 10 minutes
Servings: 4
Ingredients:

- 1 teaspoon olive oil
- ½ sweet onion, chopped
- ½ red bell pepper, chopped
- ½ teaspoon minced garlic
- 4 eggs, beaten
- ½ teaspoon ground cumin
- Pinch red pepper flakes
- 4 tortillas
- ¼ cup tomato salsa

Directions:

1. Heat the oil in a vast skillet at medium heat.
2. Add the onion, bell pepper, garlic, and sauté until softened, about 5 minutes.
3. Add the eggs, cumin, and red pepper flakes, and scramble the eggs with the vegetables until cooked through and fluffy.
4. Spoon one-fourth of the egg mixture into the center of each tortilla, and top each with 1 tablespoon of salsa.
5. Serve immediately.

Per serving: Calories: 211Kcal; Fat: 7g; Carbohydrates: 17g; Protein: 9g

5. Mexican Scrambled Eggs in Tortilla

Preparation Time: 5 minutes
Cooking Time: 2 minutes
Servings: 2
Ingredients:

- 2 medium corn tortillas
- 4 egg whites
- 1 teaspoon of cumin
- 3 teaspoons of green chilies, diced
- ½ teaspoon of hot pepper sauce
- 2 tablespoons of salsa
- ½ teaspoon salt

Directions:

1. Spray some cooking spray on a medium skillet and heat for a few seconds.
2. Whisk the eggs with the green chilies, hot sauce, and comminute
3. Add the eggs into the pan, and whisk with a spatula to scramble. Add the salt.
4. Cook until fluffy and done (1-2 minutes) over low heat.
5. Open the tortillas and spread 1 tablespoon of salsa on each.

6. Distribute the egg mixture onto the tortillas and wrap gently to make a burrito.
7. Serve warm.

Per serving: Calories: 44.1Kcal; Fat:0.39 g; Carbohydrates: 2.23g; Protein:7.69 g

6. Summer Veggie Omelet

Preparation Time: 5 minutes
Cooking Time: 5 minutes
Servings: 2
Ingredients:

- 4 large egg whites
- ¼ cup of sweet corn, frozen
- ⅓ cup of zucchini, grated
- 2 green onions, sliced
- 1 tablespoon of cream cheese
- Kosher pepper

Directions:
1. Grease a medium pan with cooking spray and add the onions, corn, and grated zucchini.
2. Sauté for a couple of minutes until softened.
3. Beat the eggs with water, cream cheese, and pepper in a bowl.
4. Add the eggs into the veggie mixture in the pan, and let cook while moving the edges from inside to outside with a spatula to allow raw eggs to cook through the borders.
5. Turn the omelet with the aid of a dish (placed over the pan, flipped upside down, and then back to the pan).
6. Let sit for another 1-2 minutes.
7. Fold in half and serve.

Per serving: Calories: 90Kcal; Fat: 2.44g; Carbohydrates: 15.97g; Protein: 8.07g

7. Sweet Pancakes

Preparation Time: 10 minutes
Cooking Time: 5 minutes
Servings: 5
Ingredients:

- All-purpose flour – 1 cup
- Granulated sugar – 1 Tablespoon
- Baking powder – 2 teaspoons.
- Egg whites – 2
- Almond milk - 1 cup
- Olive oil - 2 Tablespoons.
- Maple extract – 1 Tablespoon

Directions:
1. Combine the flour, sugar and baking powder in a bowl.
2. Make a well in the center and place it on one side.
3. Mix the egg whites, milk, oil, and maple extract in another bowl.
4. Add the egg mixture to the well and gently mix until a batter is formed.
5. Heat skillet over medium heat.
6. Cook for 2 minutes on each side or until the pancake is golden. Only add 1/5 of the batter to the pan.
7. Repeat with the remaining batter and serve.

Per serving: Calories: 178Kcal; Fat: 6g; Carbohydrates: 3g; Protein: 6g

8. Breakfast Smoothie

Preparation Time: 15 minutes
Cooking Time: 0 minute
Servings: 2
Ingredients:

- Frozen blueberries – 1 cup
- Pineapple chunks – ½ cup
- English cucumber – ½ cup
- Apple – ½

- Water – ½ cup

Directions:

1. Put the pineapple, blueberries, cucumber, apple, and water in a blender and blend until thick and smooth.
2. Pour into 2 glasses and serve.

Per serving: Calories: 87Kcal; Fat: 5g; Carbohydrates: 22g; Protein: 0.7g

9. Lean and Green Chicken Pesto Pasta

Preparation Time: 5 minutes
Cooking Time: 15 minutes
Servings: 1
Ingredients:

- 3 cups of raw kale leaves
- 2 tbsp. of olive oil
- 2 cups of fresh basil
- 1/4 teaspoon salt
- 3 tbsp. lemon juice
- Three garlic cloves
- 2 cups of cooked chicken breast
- 1 cup of baby spinach
- 6 ounces of uncooked chicken pasta
- 3 ounces of diced fresh mozzarella
- Basil leaves or red pepper flakes to garnish

Directions:

1. Start making the pesto. Add the kale, lemon juice, basil, garlic cloves, olive oil, and salt to a blender and blend until it's smooth.
2. Add salt and pepper to taste.
3. Cook the pasta and strain off the water. Reserve 1/4 cup of the liquid.
4. Get a bowl and mix the cooked pasta, pesto, diced chicken, spinach, mozzarella, and the reserved pasta liquid.

5. Sprinkle the mixture with additional chopped basil or red paper flakes (optional).
6. Now your salad is ready. You may serve it warm or chilled. Also, it can be taken as a salad mix-ins or a side dish. Leftovers should be stored in the refrigerator inside an air-tight container for 3-5 days.

Per serving: Calories:244 Kcal; Fat: 10g; Carbohydrates: 22.5g; Protein: 20.5g

10. Zucchini Egg Casserole

Preparation Time: 10 minutes
Cooking Time: 30 minutes
Servings: 8
Ingredients:

- 10 eggs
- 3 cherry tomatoes, halved
- 1/2 cup mushrooms, sliced
- 1/3 cup ham, chopped
- 1 small zucchini, sliced into rounds
- 1/2 cup spinach
- 2/3 cup Greek yogurt
- Pepper
- Salt

Directions:

1. Preheat the oven to 350 deg. F. Grease a 9*13-inch pan and set aside.
2. Whisk eggs with Greek yogurt, pepper, and salt in a large bowl. Stir in tomatoes, mushrooms, ham, zucchini, and spinach.
3. Pour egg mixture into the prepared pan and bake for 30-35 minutes.
4. Serve and enjoy.

Per serving: Calories: 134Kcal; Fat: 9.8g; Carbohydrates: 3.4g; Protein: 8.8g

11. Easy Asparagus Quiche

Preparation Time: 10 minutes
Cooking Time: 45 minutes
Servings: 8
Ingredients:

- 10 eggs
- 2 lbs. asparagus, trimmed and remove ends
- 3 tbsp olive oil
- Pepper
- Salt

Directions:

1. Preheat the oven to 425 F.
2. Arrange asparagus on the baking sheet. Drizzle 1 tablespoon olive oil over asparagus.
3. Roast asparagus in preheated oven for 15 minutes.
4. Whisk eggs with remaining oil, pepper, and salt in a mixing bowl.
5. Transfer roasted asparagus to a quiche pan. Pour egg mixture over asparagus.
6. Bake at 350 F for 30 minutes or until the egg sets.
7. Slice and serve.

Per serving: Calories: 146Kcal; Fat: 10.9g; Carbohydrates: 4.8g; Protein: 9.4g

12. Cheesy Scrambled Eggs with Fresh Herbs

Preparation Time: 15 minutes
Cooking Time: 10 minutes
Servings: 4
Ingredients:

- Eggs – 3
- Egg whites – 2
- Cream cheese – ½ cup
- Unsweetened rice milk – ¼ cup
- Chopped scallion – 1 Tablespoon green part only
- Chopped fresh tarragon – 1 Tablespoon
- Ghee – 2 Tablespoons.
- Ground black pepper to taste

Directions:

1. Mix the eggs, egg whites, cream cheese, rice milk, scallions, and tarragon in a container until mixed and smooth.
2. Melt the ghee in a skillet.
3. Pour in the egg mix, then cook for 5 minutes or until the eggs are thick and curds creamy.
4. Season with pepper and serve.

Per serving: Calories: 221Kcal; Fat: 19g; Carbohydrates: 3g; Protein: 8g

13. Turkey and Spinach Scramble on Melba Toast

Preparation Time: 2 minutes
Cooking Time: 15 minutes
Servings: 2
Ingredients:

- Extra virgin olive oil – 1 teaspoon
- Raw spinach – 1 cup
- Garlic – ½ clove, minced
- Nutmeg – 1 teaspoon grated
- Cooked and diced turkey breast – 1 cup
- Melba toast – 4 slices
- Balsamic vinegar – 1 teaspoon

Directions:

1. Heat a pot over a source of heat and add oil.
2. Add turkey and heat through for 6 to 8 minutes.
3. Add spinach, garlic, and nutmeg and stir-fry for 6 minutes more.

4. Plate up the Melba toast and top with spinach and turkey scramble.
5. Drizzle with balsamic vinegar and serve.

Per serving: Calories: 301Kcal; Fat: 19g; Carbohydrates: 12g; Protein: 19g

14. Vegetable Omelet

Preparation Time: 15 minutes
Cooking Time: 10 minutes
Servings: 3
Ingredients:

- Egg whites – 4
- Egg – 1
- Chopped fresh parsley – 2 Tablespoons.
- Water – 2 Tablespoons.
- Olive oil spray
- Chopped and boiled red bell pepper – ½ cup
- Chopped scallion – ¼ cup, both green and white parts
- Ground black pepper

Directions:

1. Whisk together the egg, egg whites, parsley, and water until well blended. Set aside.
2. Spray a skillet with olive oil spray and place over medium heat.
3. Sauté the peppers and scallion for 3 minutes or until softened.
4. Over the vegetables, you can now pour the egg and cook, swirling the skillet, for 2 minutes or until the edges start to set. Cook until set.
5. Season with black pepper and serve.

Per serving: Calories: 77Kcal; Fat: 3g; Carbohydrates: 2g; Protein: 12g

15. Mexican Style Burritos

Preparation Time: 5 minutes
Cooking Time: 15 minutes
Servings: 2
Ingredients:

- Olive oil – 1 Tablespoon
- Corn tortillas – 2
- Red onion – ¼ cup, chopped
- Red bell peppers – ¼ cup, chopped
- Red chili – ½, deseeded and chopped
- Eggs – 2
- Juice of 1 lime
- Cilantro – 1 Tablespoon chopped

Directions:

1. Turn the broiler to medium heat and place the tortillas underneath for 1 to 2 minutes on each side or until lightly toasted.
2. Remove and keep the broiler on.
3. Sauté onion, chili, and bell peppers for 5 to 6 minutes or until soft.
4. Place the eggs on top of the onions and peppers and place the skillet under the broiler for 5-6 minutes or until the eggs are cooked.
5. Serve half the eggs and vegetables on top of each tortilla and sprinkle with cilantro and lime juice to serve.

Per serving: Calories: 202Kcal; Fat:13 g; Carbohydrates: 19g; Protein: 9g

16. Clean Liver Green Juice

Preparation time: 10 minutes
Cooking time: 0 minutes
Servings: 2
Ingredients:

- 2½ C. fresh spinach
- 2 large celery stalks
- 2 large green apples, cored and sliced
- 1 medium orange, peeled, seeded, and sectioned
- 1 tbsp. fresh lime juice
- 1 tbsp. fresh lemon juice

Directions:

1. Add all ingredients to a juicer and extract the juice according to the manufacturer's directions.
2. Transfer into 2 serving glasses and stir in lime and lemon juices.
3. Serve immediately.

Per serving: Calories: 476Kcal; Fat: 40g; Carbohydrates: 33g; Protein: 6g

17. Green Tea Purifying Smoothie

Preparation time: 10 minutes
Cooking time: 0 minutes
Servings: 2
Ingredients:

- 2 C. fresh baby spinach
- 3 C. frozen green grapes
- 1 medium ripe avocado peeled, pitted and chopped
- 2 tsp. organic honey
- 1½ C. strong brewed green tea

Directions:

1. In your high-speed blender, add all ingredients and pulse until smooth.
2. Transfer into serving glasses and serve immediately.

Per serving: Calories: 476Kcal; Fat: 40g; Carbohydrates: 33g; Protein: 6g

18. Smoothie With Ginger and Cucumber

Preparation time: 10 minutes
Cooking time: 0 minutes
Servings: 2
Ingredients:

- 1 cup chilled water
- 2 slices of cucumber
- 1 tablespoon lime juice
- A couple of mint leaves
- 1 small piece of fresh ginger

Directions:

1. Add a chilled cup of water to an electric mixer, and grate the ginger piece.
2. Mix with cucumber slices, lime juice and mint leaves to serve.

Per serving: Calories: 170Kcal; Fat: 3g; Carbohydrates: 8g; Protein: 5g

19. Oatmeal Blast with Fruit

Preparation time: 10 minutes
Cooking time: 0 minutes
Servings: 2
Ingredients:

- ½ cup oats (steel cut)
- A pinch of ground cinnamon
- Ice cubes as needed
- 1 cup water
- ½ cup pineapple chunks

Directions:

1. Add oats to a blender and lightly blend with water. Add the fruit and other ingredients afterwards and mix again.

Per serving: Calories: 150Kcal; Fat: 3g; Carbohydrates: 6g; Protein: 8g

20. White Bean Smoothie

Preparation time: 10 minutes
Cooking time: 0 minutes
Servings: 2
Ingredients:

- 1 cup unsweetened rice milk (chilled)
- ¼ cup peach slices
- ¼ cup white beans cooked
- A pinch of cinnamon powder
- A pinch of nutmeg

Directions:

1. Pour milk into the blender and add other ingredients to blend till smooth enough to serve and drink.

Per serving: Calories: 150Kcal; Fat: 3g; Carbohydrates: 6g; Protein: 8g

CHAPTER 4: Snacks Recipes

21. Raw Broccoli Poppers

Preparation Time: 2 minutes
Cooking Time: 8 minutes
Servings: 4
Ingredients:

- 1/8 cup water
- 1/8 tsp. fine sea salt
- 4 cups broccoli florets, washed and cut into 1-inch pieces
- 1/4 tsp. turmeric powder
- 1 cup unsalted cashews, soaked overnight or at least 3-4 hours and drained
- 1/4 tsp. onion powder
- 1 red bell pepper, seeded and
- 2 tbsp. nutritional heaping
- 2 tbsp. lemon juice

Directions:

1. Transfer the drained cashews to a high-speed blender and pulse for about 30 seconds. Add in the chopped pepper and pulse again for 30 seconds.
2. Add 2 tbsp. of lemon juice, 1/8 cup of water, 2 tbsp. of nutritional yeast/heaping, ¼ tsp. of onion powder, 1/8 of tsp. fine sea salt, and 1/4 tsp. of turmeric powder. Pulse for about 45 seconds until smooth.
3. Handover the broccoli into a bowl and add the chopped cheesy cashew mixture. Toss well until coated.
4. Transfer the pieces of broccoli to the trays of a yeast dehydrator.
5. Follow the dehydrator's instructions and dehydrate for about 8 minutes at 125°F or until crunchy.

Per serving: Calories: 408Kcal; Fat: 32g; Carbohydrates: 22g; Protein: 15g

22. Candied Ginger

Preparation Time: 10 minutes
Cooking Time: 40 minutes
Servings: 3–5
Ingredients:

- 2 1/2 cups salted pistachios, shelled
- 1 1/4 tsp. powdered ginger
- 3 tbsp. pure maple syrup

Directions:

1. Add 1 1/4 tsp. of powdered ginger to a bowl with pistachios. Stir well until combined. There
2. Should be no lumps.
3. Drizzle with 3 tbsp. of maple syrup and stir well.
4. Transfer to your baking sheet lined with parchment paper and spread evenly.
5. Cook in a preheated oven at 275°F for about 20 minutes.
6. Take it out from the oven, stir, and cook for 10–15 minutes.
7. Let it cool for about a few minutes until crispy. Enjoy!

Per serving: Calories: 378Kcal; Fat: 27.6g; Carbohydrates: 26g; Protein: 13g

23. Chia Crackers

Preparation Time: 20 minutes
Cooking Time: 1 hour
Servings: 24–26
Ingredients:

- 1/2 cup pecans, chopped

- 1/2 cup chia seeds
- 1/2 tsp. cayenne pepper
- 1 cup water
- 1/4 cup nutritional yeast
- 1/2 cup pumpkin seeds
- 1/4 cup ground flax
- Salt and pepper to taste

Directions:

1. Mix around 1/2 cup of chia seeds and 1 cup of water. Keep it aside.
2. Take another bowl and combine all the remaining ingredients. Combine well and stir in the chia water mixture until you obtain a dough.
3. Transfer the dough onto a baking sheet and roll it out into a ¼"-thick dough.
4. Transfer into a preheated oven at 325°F and bake for about ½ hour.
5. Take it out from the oven, flip the dough, and cut it into desired cracker shaped-squares.
6. Spread and back again for half an hour, or until crispy and browned.
7. Once done, take them out from the oven and let them cool at room temperature. Enjoy!

Per serving: Calories: 41Kcal; Fat: 3.1g; Carbohydrates: 2g; Protein: 2g

24. Wheat Crackers

Preparation Time: 10 minutes
Cooking Time: 20 minutes
Servings: 4
Ingredients:

- 1 3/4 cups almond flour
- 1 1/2 cups coconut flour
- 3/4 teaspoon sea salt
- 1/3 cup vegetable oil
- 1 cup alkaline water
- Sea salt for sprinkling

Directions:

1. Set your oven to 350 deg. F.
2. Mix coconut flour, almond flour, and salt in a bowl.
3. Stir in vegetable oil and water. Mix well until smooth.
4. Spread this dough on a floured surface into a thin sheet.
5. Cut small squares out of this sheet.
6. Arrange the dough squares on a baking sheet lined with parchment paper.
7. Bake for 20 minutes until light golden.
8. Serve.

Per serving: Calories: 64Kcal; Fat: 9.2g; Carbohydrates: 9.2g; Protein: 1.5g

25. Potato Chips

Preparation Time: 10 minutes
Cooking Time: 5 minutes
Servings: 4
Ingredients:

- 1 tablespoon vegetable oil
- 1 potato, sliced paper thin
- Sea salt, to taste

Directions:

1. Toss the potato with oil and sea salt.
2. Spread the slices in a baking dish in a single layer.
3. Cook in a microwave for 5 minutes until golden brown.
4. Serve.

Per serving: Calories: 80Kcal; Fat: 3.5g; Carbohydrates: 11.6g; Protein: 1.2g

26. Rosemary & Garlic Kale Chips

Preparation Time: 10 minutes
Cooking Time: 30 minutes
Servings: 1
Ingredients:

- 9oz kale chips, chopped into 2inch
- 2 sprigs of rosemary
- 2 cloves of garlic
- 2 tablespoons olive oil
- Sea salt
- Freshly ground black pepper

Directions:

1. Gently warm the olive oil, rosemary and garlic over low heat for 10 minutes. Remove it from the heat and set it aside to cool.
2. Take the rosemary and garlic out of the oil and discard them.
3. Toss the kale leaves in the oil, ensuring they are well coated.
4. Season with salt and pepper.
5. Spread the kale leaves onto 2 baking sheets and bake them in the oven at 170C/325F for 15 minutes, until crispy.

Per serving: Calories:249 Kcal; Fat: 4.3g; Carbohydrates: 15.3g; Protein: 1.4g

27. Collard Greens and Tomatoes

Preparation Time: 10 minutes
Cooking Time: 12 minutes
Servings: 5
Ingredients:

- 1-pound collard greens
- 3 bacon strips, chopped
- ¼ cup cherry tomatoes halved
- 1 tbsp. apple cider vinegar
- 2 tbsp. chicken stock
- Salt and ground black pepper to taste

Directions:

1. Heat your pan over medium heat, add the bacon, stir, and cook until it browns. Add the tomatoes, collard greens, vinegar, stock, salt, and pepper, stir and cook for 8 minutes.
2. Add more salt and pepper, stir gently, divide onto plates, and serve.

Per serving: Calories: 120Kcal; Fat: 8g; Carbohydrates: 3g; Protein: 7g

28. Blueberry Cauliflower

Preparation Time: 2 minutes
Cooking Time: 5 minutes
Servings: 1
Ingredients:

- ¼ cup frozen strawberries
- 2 tsp. maple syrup
- ¾ cup unsweetened cashew milk
- 1 tsp. vanilla extract
- ½ cup plain cashew yogurt
- 5 tbsp. powdered peanut butter
- ¾ cup frozen wild blueberries
- ½ cup cauliflower florets, coarsely chopped

Directions:

1. Add all the smoothie ingredients to a high-speed blender.
2. Quickly combine until smooth.
3. Pour into a chilled glass and serve.

Per serving: Calories: 340Kcal; Fat:11 g; Carbohydrates: 48g; Protein: 16g

29. Roasted Asparagus

Preparation Time: 10 minutes
Cooking Time: 10 minutes
Servings: 3
Ingredients:

- 1 asparagus bunch, trimmed
- 3 tsp. avocado oil
- A splash of lemon juice
- Salt and ground black pepper to taste
- 1 tbsp. fresh oregano, chopped

Directions:

1. Spread the asparagus spears on a lined baking sheet, season with salt, and pepper, drizzle with oil and lemon juice, sprinkle with oregano and toss to coat well.
2. Put in an oven at 425°F, and bake for 10 minutes.
3. Divide onto plates and serve.

Per serving: Calories: 130Kcal; Fat: 1g; Carbohydrates: 2g; Protein: 3.4g

30. Asparagus Frittata

Preparation Time: 10 minutes
Cooking Time: 15 minutes
Servings: 4
Ingredients:

- ¼ cup onion, chopped
- Drizzle of olive oil
- 1-pound asparagus spears, cut into 1-inch pieces
- Salt and ground black pepper to taste
- 4 eggs, whisked
- 1 cup cheddar cheese, grated

Directions:

1. Heat your pan with the oil over medium-high heat, add the onions, stir, and cook for 3 minutes. Add the asparagus, stir, and cook for 6 minutes. Add the eggs, stir, and cook for 3 minutes.
2. Add the salt and pepper, sprinkle with the cheese, put in an oven, and broil for 3 minutes.
3. Divide the frittata onto plates and serve.

Per serving: Calories: 200Kcal; Fat: 12g; Carbohydrates: 5g; Protein: 14g

31. Roasted Radishes

Preparation Time: 10 minutes
Cooking Time: 35 minutes
Servings: 2
Ingredients:

- 2 cups radishes cut in quarters
- Salt and ground black pepper to taste
- 2 tbsp. butter, melted
- 1 tbsp. fresh chives, chopped
- 1 tbsp. lemon zest

Directions:

1. Spread the radishes on a lined baking sheet. Add the salt, pepper, chives, lemon zest, and butter, toss to coat, and bake in the oven at 375°F for 35 minutes.
2. Divide onto plates and serve.

Per serving: Calories: 122Kcal; Fat: 12g; Carbohydrates: 3g; Protein: 14g

32. Radish Hash Browns

Preparation Time: 10 minutes.
Cooking Time: 10 minutes
Servings: 4
Ingredients:

- ½ tsp. onion powder
- 1-pound radishes, shredded
- ½ tsp. garlic powder
- Salt and ground black pepper to taste
- 4 eggs

- ⅓ Cup Parmesan cheese, grated

Directions:

1. Mix the radishes with salt, pepper, onion, garlic powder, eggs, and Parmesan cheese in a bowl, and stir well.
2. Spread on a lined baking sheet, put in an oven at 375°F, and bake for 10 minutes.
3. Divide the hash browns onto plates and serve.

Per serving: Calories: 80Kcal; Fat: 5g; Carbohydrates: 5g; Protein: 7g

33. Strawberry Frozen Yogurt

Preparation Time: 10 minutes
Cooking Time: 15 minutes
Servings: 4
Ingredients:

- 15 ounces of plain yogurt
- 6 ounces of strawberries
- Juice of 1 orange
- 1 tablespoon honey

Directions:

1. Place the strawberries and orange juice into a food processor or blender and blitz until smooth.
2. Press the mixture through a sieve into a large bowl to remove seeds.
3. Stir in the honey and yogurt. Transfer the mixture to an ice cream maker and follow the manufacturer's instructions.
4. Alternatively, pour the mixture into a container and place it in the fridge for 1 hour. Use a fork to whisk it, break up the ice crystals, and freeze for 2 hours.

Per serving: Calories: 238Kcal; Fat: 1.8g; Carbohydrates: 12.3g; Protein: 1.3g

34. Walnut & Spiced Apple Tonic

Preparation Time: 10 minutes
Cooking Time: 15 minutes
Servings: 1
Ingredients:

- 6 walnuts halves
- 1 apple, cored
- 1 banana
- ½ teaspoon matcha powder
- ½ teaspoon cinnamon
- Pinch of ground nutmeg

Directions:

1. Place ingredients into a blender and add sufficient water to cover them. Blitz until smooth and creamy.

Per serving: Calories: 124Kcal; Fat: 2.1g; Carbohydrates: 12.3g; Protein: 1.2g

35. Basil & Walnut Pesto

Preparation Time: 10 minutes
Cooking Time: 30 minutes
Servings: 1
Ingredients:

- 2oz fresh basil
- 2oz walnuts
- 1oz pine nuts
- 3 cloves of garlic, crushed
- 2 tablespoons Parmesan, grated
- 4 tablespoons olive oil

Directions:

1. Place the pesto ingredients into a food processor and process until it becomes a smooth paste.
2. Serve with meat, fish, salad and pasta dishes.

Per serving: Calories: 136Kcal; Fat: 3.1g; Carbohydrates: 14.3g; Protein: 1.4g

36. Honey Chili Nuts

Preparation Time: 10 minutes
Cooking Time: 30 minutes
Servings: 1
Ingredients:

- 5oz walnuts
- 5oz pecan nuts
- 2oz softened butter
- 1 tablespoon honey
- ½ bird's-eye chili, very finely chopped and de-seeded

Directions:

1. Preheat the oven to 180C/360F.
2. Combine the butter, honey and chili in a bowl, then add the nuts and stir them well.
3. Spread the nuts onto a lined baking sheet and roast them in the oven for 10 minutes, stirring once halfway through.
4. Remove from the oven and allow them to cool before eating.

Per serving: Calories: 295Kcal; Fat: 4.7g; Carbohydrates: 14.6g; Protein: 1.3g

37. Mozzarella Cauliflower Bars

Preparation Time: 10 minutes
Cooking Time: 40 minutes
Servings: 12
Ingredients:

- 1 big cauliflower head, riced
- ½ cup low-fat mozzarella cheese, shredded
- ¼ cup egg whites
- 1 teaspoon Italian seasoning
- Black pepper to the taste

Directions:

1. Spread the cauliflower rice on a lined baking sheet, cook in the oven at 375 degrees F for 20 minutes, transfer to a bowl, add black pepper, cheese, seasoning, and egg whites, stir well, spread into a rectangle pan and press on the bottom.
2. Introduce in the oven at 375 degrees F, bake for 20 minutes, cut into 12 bars, and serve as a snack.

Per serving: Calories: 140Kcal; Fat: 1g; Carbohydrates: 6g; Protein: 6g

38. Grape, Celery & Parsley Reviver

Preparation Time: 10 minutes
Cooking Time: 0 minutes
Servings: 2
Ingredients:

- 3oz red grapes
- 3 sticks of celery
- 1 avocado, de-stoned and peeled
- 1 tablespoon fresh parsley
- ½ teaspoon matcha powder

Directions:

1. Place all of the ingredients into a blender with enough water to cover them and blitz until smooth and creamy.
2. Add crushed ice to make it even more refreshing.

Per serving: Calories: 334Kcal; Fat:1.5 g; Carbohydrates: 42.9g; Protein: 6g

39. Roasted Red Endive with Caper Butter

Preparation Time: 10 minutes
Cooking Time: 25 minutes
Servings: 4
Ingredients:

- 10 – 12 red endives
- 2 teaspoons extra virgin olive oil
- 2–5 anchovy fillets packed in oil
- 1 small lemon, juiced
- 3 tablespoons capers, drained
- 5 tablespoons cold butter, cut into cubes
- 1 tablespoon fresh parsley, chopped
- Salt and pepper as needed

Directions:

1. Preheat the oven to 425 deg. F.
2. Toss endives with olive oil, salt, and pepper, spread out onto a baking sheet cut side down. Bake for about 20-25 minutes or until caramelized.
3. While they're roasting, add the anchovies to a large pan over medium heat and use a fork to mash them until broken up.
4. Add lemon juice and mix well, then add capers.
5. Lower the heat and slowly stir in the butter and parsley.
6. Drizzle butter over roasted endives, season as necessary, and garnish with more fresh parsley.

Per serving: Calories: 409Kcal; Fat: 8.6g; Carbohydrates: 4.9g; Protein: 1.5g

40. Cinnamon Maple Sweet Potato Bites

Preparation Time: 5 minutes
Cooking Time: 25 minutes
Servings: 3–4
Ingredients:

- ½ tsp. corn-starch
- 1 tsp. cinnamon
- 4 medium sweet potatoes, then peeled and cut into bite-size cubes
- 2–3 tbsp. maple syrup
- 3 tbsp. butter, melted

Directions:

1. Transfer the potato cubes to a bag Ziploc® and add 3 tbsp. of melted butter. Seal and shake well until the potato cubes are coated with butter.
2. Add in the remaining ingredients and shake again.
3. Transfer the potato cubes to a parchment-lined baking sheet. The cubes shouldn't be stacked on one another.
4. Sprinkle with the cinnamon, if needed, and bake in a preheated oven at 425°F for about 25–30 minutes, stirring once during cooking.
5. Once done, take them out and stand them at room temperature. Enjoy!

Per serving: Calories: 436Kcal; Fat: 17.4g; Carbohydrates: 71.8g; Protein: 4.1g

CHAPTER 5: Salads Recipes

41. Crispy Fennel Salad

Preparation Time: 5 minutes
Cooking Time: 15 minutes
Servings: 2
Ingredients:

- 1 fennel bulb, finely sliced
- 1 grapefruit, cut into segments
- 1 orange, cut into segments
- 2 tablespoons almond slices, toasted
- 1 teaspoon chopped mint
- 1 tablespoon chopped dill
- Salt and pepper to taste
- 1 tablespoon grape seed oil

Directions:

1. Mix the fennel bulb with the grapefruit and orange segments on a platter.
2. Top with almond slices, mint and dill, drizzle with the oil, and season with salt and pepper.
3. Serve the salad as fresh as possible.

Per serving: Calories: 104Kcal; Fat: 0.5g; Carbohydrates: 25.5g; Protein: 3.1g

42. Provencal Summer Salad

Preparation Time: 5 minutes
Cooking Time: 25 minutes
Servings: 2
Ingredients:

- 1 zucchini, sliced
- 1 eggplant, sliced
- 2 red onions, sliced
- 2 tomatoes, sliced
- 1 teaspoon dried mint
- 2 garlic cloves, minced
- 2 tablespoons balsamic vinegar
- Salt and pepper to taste

Directions:

1. Season the zucchini, eggplant, onions and tomatoes with salt and pepper. Cook the vegetable slices on the grill until browned.
2. Transfer the vegetables to a salad bowl, then add the mint, garlic and vinegar.
3. Serve the salad right away.

Per serving: Calories: 74Kcal; Fat: 0.5g; Carbohydrates: 16.5g; Protein: 3g

43. Roasted Vegetable Salad

Servings: 6
Cooking Time: 30 Minutes
Ingredients:

- ½ pound of baby carrots
- 2 red onions, sliced
- 1 zucchini, sliced
- 2 eggplants, cubed
- 1 cauliflower, cut into florets
- 1 sweet potato, peeled and cubed
- 1 endive, sliced
- 3 tablespoons extra virgin olive oil
- 1 teaspoon dried basil
- Salt and pepper to taste
- 1 lemon, juiced
- 1 tablespoon balsamic vinegar

Directions:

1. Combine the vegetables with the oil, basil, salt and pepper in a deep-dish baking pan and cook in the preheated oven at 350F for 25-30 minutes.
2. When done, transfer to a salad bowl and add the lemon juice and vinegar.
3. Serve the salad fresh.

Per serving: Calories: 164Kcal; Fat: 7.6g; Carbohydrates: 24.2g; Protein: 3.7g

44. Spanish Tomato Salad

Preparation Time: 5 minutes
Cooking Time: 10 minutes
Servings: 2
Ingredients:

- 1 pound of tomatoes, cubed
- 2 cucumbers, cubed
- 2 garlic cloves, chopped
- 1 red onion, sliced
- 2 anchovy fillets
- 1 tablespoon balsamic vinegar
- 1 pinch of chili powder
- Salt and pepper to taste

Directions:

1. Combine the tomatoes, cucumbers, garlic and red onion in a bowl.
2. Mix the anchovy fillets, vinegar, chili powder, salt and pepper in a mortar.
3. Drizzle the mixture over the salad and mix well.
4. Serve the salad fresh.

Per serving: Calories: 61Kcal; Fat: 0.6g; Carbohydrates: 13g; Protein: 3g

45. Grilled Salmon Summer Salad

Preparation Time: 5 minutes
Cooking Time: 30 minutes
Servings: 2
Ingredients:

- Salmon fillets - 2
- Salt and pepper - to taste
- Vegetable stock - 2 cups
- Bulgur - 1 2 cup
- Cherry tomatoes - 1 cup, halved
- Sweet corn - 1 2 cup
- Lemon - 1, juiced

- Green olives - 1 2 cups, sliced
- Cucumber - 1, cubed
- Green onion - 1 chopped
- Red pepper - 1 chopped
- Red bell pepper - 1, cored and diced

Directions:

1. Heat a grill pan on medium and then place salmon on, seasoning with salt and pepper. Grill both sides of salmon until brown and set aside.
2. Heat stock in a saucepan until hot, add in bulgur and cook until liquid is completely soaked into bulgur.
3. Mix salmon, bulgur, and all other ingredients in a salad bowl, and again add salt and pepper, if desired, to suit your taste.
4. Serve the salad as soon as completed.

Per serving: Calories: 60Kcal; Fat: 3g; Carbohydrates: 5g; Protein: 8g

46. Garden Salad with Oranges And Olives

Preparation Time: 5 minutes
Cooking Time: 10 minutes
Servings: 2
Ingredients:

- ½ cup red wine vinegar
- 1 tbsp extra virgin olive oil
- 1 tbsp finely chopped celery
- 1 tbsp finely chopped red onion
- 16 large ripe black olives
- 2 garlic cloves
- 2 navel oranges, peeled and segmented
- 4 boneless, skinless chicken breasts, 4 oz. each
- 4 garlic cloves, minced
- 8 cups leaf lettuce, washed and dried
- Cracked black pepper to taste

Directions:

1. Prepare the dressing by mixing the pepper, celery, onion, olive oil, garlic and vinegar in a small bowl. Whisk well to combine.
2. Lightly grease the grate and preheat the grill to high.
3. Rub chicken with the garlic cloves and discard the garlic.
4. Grill chicken for 5 minutes per side or until cooked through.
5. Remove from grill and let it stand for 5 minutes before cutting into ½-inch strips.
6. On 4 serving plates, evenly arrange two cups of lettuce, ¼ of the sliced oranges and 4 olives per plate.
7. Top each dish with ¼ serving of grilled chicken, evenly drizzle with dressing, serve and enjoy.

Per serving: Calories: 259.8Kcal; Fat: 1.4g; Carbohydrates: 12.9g; Protein: 48.9g

47. Salmon & Arugula Salad

Preparation Time: 5 minutes
Cooking Time: 10 minutes
Servings: 2
Ingredients:

- ¼ cup red onion, sliced thinly
- 1 ½ tbsp fresh lemon juice
- 1 ½ tbsp olive oil
- 1 tbsp extra-virgin olive oil
- 1 tbsp red-wine vinegar
- 2 center-cut salmon fillets (6-oz each)
- 2/3 cup cherry tomatoes, halved
- 3 cups of baby arugula leaves
- Pepper and salt to taste

Directions:

1. Mix pepper, salt, 1 ½ tbsp olive oil, and lemon juice in a shallow bowl. Toss in salmon fillets and rub with the marinade. Allow marinating for at least 15 minutes.
2. Grease a baking sheet and preheat the oven to 350ºF.
3. Bake marinated salmon fillet for 10 to 12 minutes or until flaky with skin side touching the baking sheet.
4. Meanwhile, in a salad bowl, mix onion, tomatoes, and arugula.
5. Season with pepper and salt. Drizzle with vinegar and oil. Toss to combine and serve right away with baked salmon on the side.

Per serving: Calories: 400Kcal; Fat: 25.6g; Carbohydrates: 5.8g; Protein: 36.6g

48. Chicken Salad

Preparation Time: 5 minutes
Cooking Time: 10 minutes
Servings: 2
Ingredients:

- 1 cup buffalo sauce
- 1 tablespoon honey
- 1 tsp lime
- 1 tsp salt
- 1 tsp onion powder
- 1 tablespoon olive oil
- 1 cup salad dressing

Directions:

1. In a bowl, combine all ingredients and mix well
2. Add dressing and serve

Per serving: Calories: 44Kcal; Fat: 3g; Carbohydrates: 4.4g; Protein: 8.4g

49. Farro Salad

Preparation Time: 5 minutes
Cooking Time: 10 minutes
Servings: 2
Ingredients:

- 1 cup farro
- 1 bay leaf
- 1 shallot
- ¼ cup olive oil
- 1 tablespoon apple cider vinegar
- 1 tsp honey
- 1 cup arugula
- 1 apple
- ¼ cup basil
- ¼ cup parsley

Directions:

1. In a bowl, combine all ingredients and mix well
2. Add dressing and serve

Per serving: Calories: 69Kcal; Fat: 6.5g; Carbohydrates: 10.6g; Protein: 9.4g

50. Carrot Salad

Preparation Time: 5 minutes
Cooking Time: 10 minutes
Servings: 2
Ingredients:

- 1 lb. carrots
- 1 cup raisins
- ½ cup peanuts
- ½ cup cilantro
- 2 green onions
- ¼ cup olive oil
- 1 tablespoon honey
- 2 cloves garlic
- 1 tsp cumin

Directions:

1. In a bowl, combine all ingredients and mix well
2. Add dressing and serve

Per serving: Calories: 41Kcal; Fat: 6g; Carbohydrates: 9.6g; Protein: 11g

51. Beets Steamed Edamame Salad

Preparation time: 15 minutes
Cooking time: 5 minutes
Servings: 8
Ingredients:

- 2 bags of steamed edamame beans
- White vinegar
- 20-24 oz. can of beets
- 4 teaspoons of olive oil of high quality
- 12 large organic carrots, cubed
- 6 corn on the cobs, corn cut off
- Black pepper
- 1 pound of green beans cut into 1-inch segments

Directions:

1. Wet a paper towel and wrap the corn with the damp towel; place the wrapped corn in the microwave for 5 minutes.
2. Steam the entire ingredients (reserving corn and beets) in a large steamer in this other; carrots cubes, green beans, and edamame beans on the top layer.
3. Mix beets together with the cooked corn and cooked vegetables.
4. Toss salad slightly with a few dashes of black pepper, white vinegar, and olive oil.

Per serving: Calories: 317Kcal; Fat: 36.5g; Carbohydrates: 17.6g; Protein: 17.4g

52. Toasted Mango Pepitas Kale Salad

Preparation time: 20 minutes
Cooking time: 0 minutes
Servings: 8
Ingredients:

- 4 tsps. of honey
- 2 fresh mangoes, thinly diced (about 1 cup)
- Freshly ground black pepper
- 4 full tbsp of toasted pepitas
- Kosher salt
- One lemon juice
- 2 large bunch of kale de-stalk and sliced into ribbons
- 1/2 cup of extra-virgin olive oil, plus more

Directions:

1. Add the sliced kale into a large mixing bowl; add half the lemon juice and little salt.
2. Start working on the kale using your fingertips for five minutes or until the kale leaves are tender and sweet.
3. Spread olive oil over the kale and work on the kale with your finger for a few more minutes. Set aside.
4. Blend the black pepper and honey with the remaining half lemon juice in a small bowl.
5. Steadily drip in 1/2 cup of olive oil while whisking until it forms a dressing. Season dressing with a pinch of salt.
6. Pour a few dressings on the kale, and add the pepitas and mango. Toss together and serve.

Per serving: Calories:54 Kcal; Fat:21 g; Carbohydrates: 12g; Protein: 15g

53. Chickpea And Parsley Pumpkin Salad

Preparation time: 5 minutes
Cooking time: 10 minutes
Servings: 6
Ingredients:

- 1 1/2 small thinly sliced red onion
- 1 1/2 handful parsley, chopped
- 1 1/2 diced avocado
- 1 1/2 tbsp of lemon juice
- 1 1/2 tsp of ground coriander
- 1 1/2 tsp of ground cumin
- Salt and pepper to season
- 3 tbsp of olive oil
- 1 1/2 cup of pumpkin, peeled and chopped into bite pieces
- 1 1/2 (21.5 oz) can of chickpeas, rinsed and drained

Directions:

1. Season the pumpkin with a drizzle of olive oil, coriander and cumin.
2. Arrange seasoned pumpkin in an oven tray lined with parchment paper.
3. Roast until the pumpkin is lightly browned and soft.
4. Combine the salad ingredients into a bowl and drizzle in lemon juice.

Per serving: Calories: 53Kcal; Fat: 3g; Carbohydrates: 2g; Protein: 24g

54. Springtime Chicken Berries Salad

Preparation time: 5 minutes
Cooking time: 5 minutes
Servings: 8
Ingredients:
Salad:

- 4 cups of quartered strawberries
- 2/3 cup of vertically sliced red onion
- 2 cups of fresh blueberries
- 24 oz of boneless, skinless, rotisserie chicken breast, sliced
- 8 cups of arugula
- 8 cups of torn romaine lettuce

Dressing:

- 2 tbsp of water
- 2/8 tsps. of freshly ground black pepper
- 2/8 tsps. of salt
- 4 tbsp of extra-virgin olive oil
- 4 tbsp of red wine vinegar
- 2 tbsp of low-carb sweetener of your choice

Directions:

1. In a large mixing bowl, combine the blueberries, strawberries, arugula, romaine and onions. Toss gently to combine.
2. Combine 2 tbsp of water, black pepper, red wine vinegar salt and sweetener in a small bowl. Fold in the olive oil, often stirring, until well incorporated.
3. Arrange eight different plates and place up to 2 cups of chicken mixture on each. Drizzle with 4 teaspoons of the dressing.

Per serving: Calories: 31Kcal; Fat: 3g; Carbohydrates: 2g; Protein: 8g

55. Toaster Almond Spiralized Beet Salad

Preparation time: 15 minutes
Cooking time: 15 minutes
Servings: 4
Ingredients:

- 1/8 teaspoon of ground pepper
- 1/8 cup of extra-virgin olive oil
- 1/4 teaspoon of freshly grated lemon zest
- 1 pounds beets (2 medium)
- 1/4 cup of (fresh) chopped flat-leaf parsley
- 1 tablespoon of lemon juice
- 1/4 cup of slivered almonds, toasted
- 1/4 teaspoon of salt
- 1/6 cup of minced shallot

Directions:

1. Mix the minced shallot, lemon juice, oil, salt, pepper and lemon zest into a small bowl. Mix gently to combine, then set aside.
2. Peel the beets with a thin blade, then spiralize and cut into 3-inch lengths.
3. Arrange the spiralized beets into a large bowl. Sprinkle beets on top with the dressing, and toss gently to ensure the salad is finely coated.
4. Add chopped parsley and almonds before serving. Toss to coat.

Per serving: Calories: 97Kcal; Fat: 21g; Carbohydrates: 8g; Protein: 19.2g

56. Watercress Salad

Preparation Time: 10 minutes
Cooking Time: 4 minutes
Servings: 2
Ingredients:

- 2 cups asparagus, chopped
- 16 ounces shrimp, cooked
- 4 cups watercress, torn
- 1 tablespoon apple cider vinegar
- ¼ cup olive oil

Directions:
1. In the mixing bowl, mix up asparagus, shrimps, watercress, and olive oil.

Per serving: Calories: 264Kcal; Fat:14.8 g; Carbohydrates: 4.5g; Protein: 28.3g

57. Seafood Arugula Salad

Preparation Time: 5 minutes
Cooking Time: 10 minutes
Servings: 2
Ingredients:

- 1 tablespoon olive oil
- 2 cups shrimps, cooked
- 1 cup arugula
- 1 tablespoon cilantro, chopped

Directions:
1. Put all ingredients in your salad bowl and shake well.

Per serving: Calories: 61Kcal; Fat: 3.7g; Carbohydrates: 0.2g; Protein: 6.6g

58. Smoked Salad

Preparation Time: 10 minutes
Cooking Time: 0 minutes
Servings: 2
Ingredients:

- 1 mango, chopped
- 4 cups lettuce, chopped
- 8 oz smoked turkey, chopped
- 2 tablespoons low-fat yogurt
- 1 teaspoon smoked paprika

Directions:
1. Mix all ingredients in your bowl and transfer them to the serving plates.

Per serving: Calories:88 Kcal; Fat: 1.9g; Carbohydrates: 11.2g; Protein: 7.1g

59. Avocado Salad

Preparation Time: 5 minutes
Cooking Time: 0 minutes
Servings: 2
Ingredients:

- ½ teaspoon ground black pepper
- 1 avocado, peeled, pitted, and sliced
- 4 cups lettuce, chopped
- 1 cup black olives, pitted and halved
- 1 cup tomatoes, chopped
- 1 tablespoon olive oil

Directions:
1. Put all ingredients in your salad bowl and mix up well.

Per serving: Calories:197 Kcal; Fat: 17.1g; Carbohydrates: 10g; Protein: 1.9g

60. Berry Salad with Shrimps

Preparation Time: 7 minutes
Cooking Time: 0 minutes
Servings: 2
Ingredients:

- 1 cup corn kernels, cooked
- 1 endive, shredded
- 1 pound shrimp, cooked
- 1 tablespoon lime juice
- 2 cups raspberries, halved
- 2 tablespoons olive oil
- 1 tablespoon parsley, chopped

Directions:

1. Put all ingredients from the list above in your salad bowl and shake well.

Per serving: Calories: 283Kcal; Fat: 10.1g; Carbohydrates: 21.2g; Protein: 29.5g

CHAPTER 6: Grains Recipes

61. Bell Peppers 'N Tomato-Chickpea Rice

Preparation time: 10 minutes
Cooking time: 35 minutes
Servings: 4
Ingredients:

- 2 tablespoons olive oil
- 1/2 chopped red bell pepper
- 1/2 chopped green bell pepper
- 1/2 chopped yellow pepper
- 1/2 chopped red pepper
- 1 medium onion, chopped
- 1 clove of garlic, minced
- 2 cups cooked jasmine rice
- 1 teaspoon tomato paste
- 1 cup chickpeas
- salt to taste
- 1/2 teaspoon paprika
- 1 small tomato, chopped
- Parsley for garnish

Directions:
1. Whisk well olive oil, garlic, tomato paste, and paprika in a large mixing bowl. Season with salt generously.
2. Mix in rice and toss well to coat in the dressing.
3. Add remaining ingredients and toss well to mix.
4. Let salad rest to allow flavors to mix for 15 minutes.
5. Toss one more time and adjust the salt to taste if needed.
6. Garnish with parsley and serve.

Per serving: Calories: 490Kcal; Fat: 8.0g Carbohydrates: 93.0g; Protein: 10.0g

62. Fennel Wild Rice Risotto

Preparation Time: 5 minutes
Cooking Time: 35 minutes
Servings: 6
Ingredients:

- 2 tablespoons extra virgin olive oil
- 1 shallot, chopped
- 2 garlic cloves, minced
- 1 fennel bulb, chopped
- 1 cup wild rice
- ¼ cup dry white wine
- 2 cups chicken stock
- 1 teaspoon grated orange zest
- Salt and pepper to taste

Directions:
1. Heat the oil in a heavy saucepan.
2. Add the garlic, shallot and fennel and cook for a few minutes until softened.
3. Stir in the rice and cook for 2 additional minutes, then add the wine, stock and orange zest, with salt and pepper to taste.
4. Cook on low heat for 20 minutes.
5. Serve the risotto warm and fresh.

Per serving: Calories: 162Kcal; Fat: 2g Carbohydrates: 20g; Protein: 8g

63. Wild Rice Prawn Salad

Preparation Time: 5 minutes
Cooking Time: 35 minutes
Servings: 6
Ingredients:

- ¾ cup wild rice
- 1¾ cups chicken stock
- 1 pound prawns

- Salt and pepper to taste
- 2 tablespoons lemon juice
- 2 tablespoons extra virgin olive oil
- 2 cups arugula

Directions:

1. Combine the rice and chicken stock in a saucepan and cook until the liquid is absorbed.
2. Transfer the rice to a salad bowl.
3. Season the prawns with salt and pepper and drizzle them with lemon juice and oil.
4. Heat a grill pan over medium flame.
5. Place the prawns on the hot pan and cook on each side for 2-3 minutes.
6. For the salad, combine the rice with arugula and prawns and mix well.
7. Serve the salad fresh.

Per serving: Calories: 207Kcal; Fat: 4g Carbohydrates: 17g; Protein: 20.6g

64. Apple Oatmeal

Preparation time: 10 minutes
Cooking time: 8 minutes
Servings: 3
Ingredients:

- 1/2 tsp ground cinnamon
- 4 tbsp. fat-free vanilla yogurt
- 1 1/2 cups quick oats
- 1/4 cup maple syrup
- 3 cups apple juice
- 1/4 cup raisins
- 1/2 cup chopped apple
- 1/4 cup chopped walnuts

Directions:

1. Combine your cinnamon and apple juice in a saucepan and allow to boil.
2. Stir in your raisins, maple syrup, apples and oats.

3. Switch the heat to low and cook while stirring until most juice is absorbed. Fold in walnuts, serve and top with yogurt.

Per serving: Calories: 242Kcal; Fat: 12g Carbohydrates: 25g; Protein: 13g

65. Raspberry Overnight Porridge

Preparation Time: Overnight
Cooking Time: 0 minute
Servings: 12
Ingredients:

- ⅓ cup of rolled oats
- ½ cup almond milk
- 1 tablespoon of honey
- 5-6 raspberries, fresh or canned and unsweetened
- ⅓ cup of rolled oats
- ½ cup almond milk
- 1 tablespoon of honey
- 5-6 raspberries, fresh or canned and unsweetened

Directions:

1. Combine the oats, almond milk, and honey in a mason jar and place in the fridge overnight.
2. Serve the following day with the raspberries on top.

Per serving: Calories: 143.6Kcal; Fat: 3.91g Carbohydrates: 34.62g; Protein: 3.44g

66. Buckwheat and Grapefruit Porridge

Preparation Time: 5 minutes
Cooking Time: 20 minutes
Servings: 2
Ingredients:

- Buckwheat – ½ cup
- Grapefruit – ¼ chopped

- Honey – 1 Tablespoon
- Almond milk – 1 ½ cups
- Water – 2 cups

Directions:

1. Boil water on the stove. Add the buckwheat and place the lid on the pan.
2. Simmer for 7 to 10 minutes, in a low heat. Check to ensure water does not dry out.
3. Remove and set aside for 5 minutes, do this when most of the water is absorbed.
4. Drain excess water from the pan and stir in almond milk, heating through for 5 minutes.
5. Add the honey and grapefruit.
6. Serve.

Per serving: Calories: 231Kcal; Fat: 4g Carbohydrates: 43g; Protein: 24.2g

67. Cherry Berry Bulgur Bowl

Preparation Time: 15 minutes
Cooking Time: 15 minutes
Servings: 4
Ingredients:

- 1 cup medium-grind bulgur
- 2 cups water
- Pinch salt
- 1 cup halved and pitted cherries or 1 cup canned cherries, drained
- ½ cup raspberries
- ½ cup blackberries
- 1 tablespoon cherry jam
- 2 cups plain whole-milk yogurt

Directions:

1. Mix the bulgur, water, and salt in a medium saucepan. Do this in medium heat. Bring to a boil.

2. Reduce the heat to low, then simmer, partially covered, for 12 to 15 minutes or until the bulgur is almost tender. Cover, and let stand for 5 minutes to finish cooking. Do this after removing the pan from the heat.
3. While the bulgur is cooking, combine the raspberries and blackberries in a medium bowl. Stir the cherry jam into the fruit.
4. When the bulgur is tender, divide it among four bowls. Top each bowl with ½ cup of yogurt and an equal amount of the berry mixture and serve.

Per serving: Calories: 242Kcal; Fat: 6g Carbohydrates: 44g; Protein: 9g

68. Baked Curried Apple Oatmeal Cups

Preparation Time: 10 minutes
Cooking Time: 20 minutes
Servings: 6
Ingredients:

- 3½ cups old-fashioned oats
- 3 tablespoons brown sugar
- 2 teaspoons of your preferred curry powder
- ⅛ teaspoon salt
- 1 cup unsweetened almond milk
- 1 cup unsweetened applesauce
- 1 teaspoon vanilla
- ½ cup chopped walnuts

Directions:

1. Preheat the oven to 375°F.
2. Spray a 12-cup muffin tin with baking spray, then set aside.
3. Combine the oats, brown sugar, curry powder, and salt in a medium bowl.
4. Mix the milk, applesauce, and vanilla in a small bowl,

5. Stir the liquid ingredients into the dry ingredients and mix until just combined. Stir in the walnuts.

6. Divide the mixture among the muffin cups using a scant ⅓ cup for each.

7. Bake this for 18 to 20 minutes until the oatmeal is firm. Serve.

Per serving: Calories: 296Kcal; Fat: 10g Carbohydrates: 45g; Protein: 8g

69. Crunchy Quinoa Meal

Preparation Time: 5 minutes
Cooking Time: 25 minutes
Servings: 2
Ingredients:

- 3 cups coconut milk
- 1 cup rinsed quinoa
- 1/8 tsp. ground cinnamon
- 1 cup raspberry
- 1/2 cup chopped coconuts

Directions:

1. In a saucepan, pour milk and bring to a boil over moderate heat.

2. Add the quinoa to the milk, and then bring it to a boil once more.

3. Then, let it simmer for at least 15 minutes on medium heat until the milk is reduced.

4. Stir in the cinnamon, then mix properly.

5. Cover it, then cook for 8 minutes until the milk is completely absorbed.

6. Add the raspberry and cook the meal for 30 seconds.

7. Serve and enjoy.

Per serving: Calories: 271Kcal; Fat: 3.7g Carbohydrates: 54g; Protein: 6.5g

70. Banana Quinoa

Preparation time: 10 minutes
Cooking time: 12 minutes
Servings: 4
Ingredients:

- 1 cup quinoa
- 2 cup milk
- 1 teaspoon vanilla extract
- 1 teaspoon honey
- 2 bananas, sliced
- ¼ teaspoon ground cinnamon

Directions:

1. Pour milk into the saucepan and add quinoa.

2. Close the lid and cook it over medium heat for 12 minutes or until quinoa will absorb all liquid.

3. Chill the quinoa for about 10-15 minutes and place in the serving mason jars.

4. Add honey, vanilla extract, and ground cinnamon.

5. Stir well.

6. Top quinoa with banana and stir it before serving.

Per serving: Calories: 279Kcal; Fat: 5.3g Carbohydrates: 48.4g; Protein: 10.7g

71. Quinoa And Potato Bowl

Preparation time: 10 minutes
Cooking time: 20 minutes
Servings: 4
Ingredients:

- 1 sweet potato, peeled, chopped
- 1 tablespoon olive oil
- ½ teaspoon chili flakes
- ½ teaspoon salt
- 1 cup quinoa
- 2 cups of water

- 1 teaspoon butter
- 1 tablespoon fresh cilantro, chopped

Directions:
1. Line the baking tray with parchment.
2. Arrange the chopped sweet potato in the tray and sprinkle it with chili flakes, salt, and olive oil.
3. Bake the sweet potato for 20 minutes at 355F.
4. Meanwhile, pour water into the saucepan.
5. Add quinoa and cook it over medium heat for 7 minutes or until quinoa will absorb all liquid.
6. Add butter to the cooked quinoa and stir well.
7. Transfer it to the bowls, and add baked sweet potato and chopped cilantro.

Per serving: Calories: 221Kcal; Fat: 7.1g Carbohydrates: 33.2g; Protein: 6.6g

72. Seeds And Lentils Oats

Preparation time: 10 minutes
Cooking time: 50 minutes
Servings: 4
Ingredients:

- ½ cup red lentils
- ¼ cup pumpkin seeds, toasted
- 2 teaspoons olive oil
- ¼ cup rolled oats
- ¼ cup coconut flesh, shredded
- 1 tablespoon honey
- 1 tablespoon orange zest, grated
- 1 cup Greek yogurt
- 1 cup blackberries

Directions:
1. Spread the lentils on a baking sheet lined with parchment paper, introduce them to the oven, and roast at 370 degrees F for 30 minutes.

2. Add the rest of the ingredients except the yoghurt and the berries, toss and bake at 370 degrees F for 20 minutes more.
3. Transfer this to a bowl, add the rest of the ingredients, toss, divide into smaller bowls and serve for breakfast.

Per serving: Calories: 204Kcal; Fat: 7.1g Carbohydrates: 27.6g; Protein: 9.5g

73. Couscous With Artichokes, Sun-dried Tomatoes, And Feta

Preparation time: 10 minutes
Cooking time: 20 minutes
Servings: 46
Ingredients:

- 3 cups chicken breast, cooked, chopped
- 2 1/3 cups water, divided
- 2 jars (6 ounces each) of marinated artichoke hearts, undrained
- 1/4 teaspoon black pepper, freshly ground
- 1/2 cup tomatoes, sun-dried
- 1/2 cup (2 ounces) feta cheese, crumbled
- 1 cup flat-leaf parsley, fresh, chopped
- 1 3/4 cups whole-wheat Israeli couscous, uncooked
- 1 can (14 1/2 ounces) vegetable broth

Directions:
1. In a microwavable bowl, combine 2 cups of the water and the tomatoes. Microwave on HIGH for about 3 minutes or until the water boils. When water is boiling, remove from the microwave, cover, and let stand for about 3 minutes or until the tomatoes are soft; drain, chop, and set aside.

2. In a large saucepan, place the vegetable broth and the remaining 1/3 cup of water; bring to boil. Stir in the couscous, cover, reduce heat, and simmer for about 8 minutes or until tender.
3. Remove your pan from the heat; add the tomatoes and the remaining ingredients. Stir to combine.

Per serving: Calories: 419Kcal; Fat: 14.1g Carbohydrates: 42.5g; Protein: 30.2g

74. Cinnamon Roll Oats

Preparation time: 10 minutes
Cooking time: 10 minutes
Servings: 4
Ingredients:

- ½ cup rolled oats
- 1 cup milk
- 1 teaspoon vanilla extract
- 1 teaspoon ground cinnamon
- 2 teaspoon honey
- 2 tablespoons Plain yogurt
- 1 teaspoon butter

Directions:

1. Pour milk into the saucepan. Bring it to a boil.
2. Add rolled oats and stir well.
3. Close the lid and simmer the oats for 5 minutes over medium heat. The cooked oats will absorb all milk.
4. Then add butter and stir the oats well.
5. Whisk together Plain yogurt with honey, cinnamon, and vanilla extract in the separated bowl.
6. Transfer the cooked oats to the serving bowls.
7. Top the oats with the yogurt mixture in the shape of the wheel.

Per serving: Calories: 243Kcal; Fat: 20.2g Carbohydrates: 2.8g; Protein: 13.3g

75. Spinach Wrap

Preparation time: 10 minutes
Cooking time: 10 minutes
Servings: 4
Ingredients:

- 4 pieces (10-inch) spinach wraps (or whole wheat tortilla or sun-dried tomato wraps)
- 1 pound chicken tenders
- 1 cup cucumber, chopped
- 3 tablespoons extra-virgin olive oil
- 1 medium tomato, chopped
- 1/3 cup couscous, whole-wheat
- 2 teaspoons garlic, minced
- 1/4 teaspoon salt, divided
- 1/4 teaspoon freshly ground pepper
- 1/4 cup lemon juice
- 1/2 cup water
- 1/2 cup fresh mint, chopped
- 1 cup fresh parsley, chopped

Directions:

1. In a small saucepan, pour the water and bring it to a boil. Stir in the couscous, remove the pan from heat, cover, and allow to stand for 5 minutes, then fluff using a fork; set aside.
2. Meanwhile, in a small mixing bowl, combine the mint, parsley, oil, lemon juice, garlic, 1/8 teaspoon of salt, and pepper.
3. In your medium mixing bowl, toss the chicken with 1 tablespoon of the mint mixture and the remaining 1/8 teaspoon of salt.
4. Place the chicken mixture into a large non-stick skillet; cook for about 3-5

minutes on each side, or until heated through. Remove from the skillet, allow to cool enough to handle, and cut into bite-sized pieces.

5. Stir the remaining mint mixture, the cucumber, and the tomato into the couscous.

6. Spread about 3/4 cup of the couscous mix onto each wrap, divide the chicken between the wraps, roll like a burrito, and tuck the sides in to hold to secure the ingredients. Cut in halves and serve.

Per serving: Calories: 479Kcal; Fat: 17g Carbohydrates: 49g; Protein: 15g

76. Peanut Butter and Cacao Breakfast Quinoa

Preparation Time: 5 minutes
Cooking Time: 10 minutes
Servings: 1
Ingredients:

- 1/3 cup quinoa flakes
- 1/2 cup unsweetened nondairy milk,
- 1/2 cup of water
- 1/8 cup raw cacao powder
- One tablespoon of natural creamy peanut butter
- 1/8 teaspoon ground cinnamon
- One banana, mashed
- Fresh berries of choice for serving
- Chopped nuts of choice for serving

Directions:

1. Using an 8-quart pot over medium-high heat, stir together the quinoa flakes, milk, water, cacao powder, peanut butter, and cinnamon. Cook and stir until the mixture begins to simmer. Turn the heat to medium-low and cook for 3 to 5 minutes, stirring frequently.

2. Stir in the bananas and cook until hot.

3. Serve topped with fresh berries, nuts, and a splash of milk.

Per serving: Calories: 471Kcal; Fat: 16g Carbohydrates: 69g; Protein: 18g

77. Orzo And Veggie Bowls

Preparation time: 10 minutes
Cooking time: 0 minutes
Servings: 4
Ingredients:

- 2 and ½ cups whole-wheat orzo, cooked
- 14 ounces canned beans, drained and rinsed
- 1 yellow bell pepper, cubed
- 1 green bell pepper, cubed
- A pinch of salt and black pepper
- 3 tomatoes, cubed
- 1 red onion, chopped
- 1 cup mint, chopped
- 2 cups feta cheese, crumbled
- 2 tablespoons olive oil
- ¼ cup lemon juice
- 1 tablespoon lemon zest, grated
- 1 cucumber, cubed
- 1 and ¼ cup kalamata olives, pitted and sliced
- 3 garlic cloves, minced

Directions:

1. In a salad bowl, combine the orzo with the beans, bell peppers, and the ingredients, toss, divide the mix between plates and serve for breakfast.

Per serving: Calories: 411Kcal; Fat: 17g Carbohydrates: 51g; Protein: 14g

78. Vanilla Oats

Preparation time: 10 minutes
Cooking time: 10 minutes
Servings: 4
Ingredients:

- ½ cup rolled oats
- 1 cup milk
- 1 teaspoon vanilla extract
- 1 teaspoon ground cinnamon
- 2 teaspoon honey
- 2 tablespoons Plain yogurt
- 1 teaspoon butter

Directions:

1. Pour milk into the saucepan and bring it to a boil.
2. Add rolled oats and stir well.
3. Close the lid and simmer the oats for 5 minutes over medium heat. The cooked oats will absorb all milk.
4. Then add butter and stir the oats well.
5. Whisk together Plain yogurt with honey, cinnamon, and vanilla extract in the separated bowl.
6. Transfer the cooked oats to the serving bowls.
7. Top the oats with the yogurt mixture in the shape of the wheel.

Per serving: Calories: 243Kcal; Fat:20.2 g Carbohydrates: 2.8g; Protein: 13.3g

79. Mint Quinoa

Preparation Time: 5 minutes
Cooking Time: 10 minutes
Servings: 2
Ingredients:

- 1 cup quinoa
- 1 ¼ cup of water
- 4 teaspoons lemon juice
- ¼ teaspoon garlic clove, diced
- 5 tablespoons sesame oil
- 2 cucumbers, chopped
- 1/3 teaspoon ground black pepper
- 1/3 cup tomatoes, chopped
- ½ oz scallions, chopped
- ¼ teaspoon fresh mint, chopped

Directions:

1. Pour water into the pan. Add quinoa and boil it for 10 minutes.
2. Then close the lid and let it rest for 5 minutes more.
3. Meanwhile, mix up lemon juice, diced garlic, sesame oil, cucumbers, ground black pepper, tomatoes, scallions, and fresh mint in the mixing bowl.
4. Then add cooked quinoa and carefully mix the side dish with the help of a spoon.
5. Store tabbouleh for up to 2 days in the fridge.

Per serving: Calories:168 Kcal; Fat: 9.9g Carbohydrates: 16.9g; Protein: 3.6g

80. Brown Rice Pilaf With Butternut Squash

Preparation time: 10 minutes
Cooking time: 50 minutes
Servings: 3
Ingredients:

- Pepper to taste
- A pinch of cinnamon
- 1 tsp salt
- 2 tbsp chopped fresh oregano
- ½ cup chopped fennel fronds
- ½ cup white wine
- 1 ¾ cups water + 2 tbsp, divided
- 1 cup instant or parboiled brown rice
- 1 tbsp tomato paste
- 1 garlic clove, minced

- 1 large onion, finely chopped
- 3 tbsp extra virgin olive oil
- 2 lbs. butternut squash, peeled, halved & seeded

Directions:

1. In a large hole grater, grate squash.
2. Place a large nonstick skillet on medium-low fire and heat oil for 2 minutes.
3. Add garlic and onions. Sauté for 8 minutes or until lightly colored and soft.
4. Add 2 tbsp water and tomato paste. Stir well to combine, then cook for 3 minutes.
5. Add rice, mix well to coat the mixture, and cook for 5 minutes while stirring frequently.
6. If needed, add squash in batches until it has wilted so you can cover the pan.
7. Add remaining water and increase the fire to medium-high.
8. Add wine, cover, and boil. Once boiling, lower fire to a simmer, then cook for 20 to 25 minutes or until liquid is fully absorbed.
9. Stir in pepper, cinnamon, salt, oregano, and fennel fronds.
10. Turn off the fire, cover and let it stand for 5 minutes before serving.

Per serving: Calories:147 Kcal; Fat: 5.5g Carbohydrates: 22.1g; Protein: 2.3g

CHAPTER 7: Meat Recipes

81. Chicken with Potatoes, Olives & Sprouts

Preparation Time: 15 minutes
Cooking Time: 35 minutes
Servings: 4
Ingredients:

- 1 lb. chicken breasts, skinless, boneless, and cut into pieces
- ¼ cup olives, quartered
- 1 tsp oregano
- 1 ½ tsp Dijon mustard
- 1 lemon juice
- 1/3 cup vinaigrette dressing
- 1 medium onion, diced
- 3 cups of potatoes cut into pieces
- 4 cups Brussels sprouts, trimmed and quartered
- ¼ tsp pepper
- ¼ tsp salt

Directions:

1. Warm-up oven to 400 F. Place chicken in the center of the baking tray, then place potatoes, sprouts, and onions around the chicken.
2. Mix vinaigrette, oregano, mustard, lemon juice, and salt in a small bowl and pour over chicken and veggies. Sprinkle olives and season with pepper.
3. Bake in preheated oven for 20 minutes. Transfer chicken to a plate. Stir the vegetables and roast for 15 minutes more. Serve and enjoy.

Per serving: Calories: 397kcal; Fat: 13g; Carbohydrates:31.4 g; Protein: 38.3g

82. Garlic Mushroom Chicken

Preparation Time: 15 minutes
Cooking Time: 15 minutes
Servings: 4
Ingredients:

- 4 chicken breasts, boneless and skinless
- 3 garlic cloves, minced
- 1 onion, chopped
- 2 cups mushrooms, sliced
- 1 tbsp olive oil
- ½ cup chicken stock
- ¼ tsp pepper
- ½ tsp salt

Directions:

1. Season chicken with pepper and salt. Warm oil in a pan on medium heat, then put seasoned chicken in the pan and cook for 5-6 minutes on each side. Remove and place on a plate.
2. Add onion and mushrooms to the pan and sauté until tender, about 2-3 minutes. Add garlic and sauté for a minute. Add stock and bring to boil. Stir well and cook for 1-2 minutes. Pour over the chicken and serve.

Per serving: Calories: 331kcal; Fat: 14.5g; Carbohydrates: 4.6g; Protein: 43.9g

83. Grilled Chicken

Preparation Time: 15 minutes
Cooking Time: 15 minutes
Servings: 4
Ingredients:

- 4 chicken breasts, skinless and boneless
- 1 ½ tsp dried oregano
- 1 tsp paprika
- 5 garlic cloves, minced
- ½ cup fresh parsley, minced
- ½ cup olive oil
- ½ cup fresh lemon juice
- Pepper
- Salt

Directions:

1. Add lemon juice, oregano, paprika, garlic, parsley, and olive oil to a large zip-lock bag. Season chicken with pepper and salt and add to bag. Seal bag and shake well to coat chicken with marinade. Let sit chicken in the marinade for 20 minutes.
2. Remove chicken from marinade and grill over medium-high heat for 5-6 minutes on each side. Serve and enjoy.

Per serving: Calories: 512kcal; Fat:36.5 g; Carbohydrates: 3g; Protein: 43.1g

84. Oat Risotto With Mushrooms, Kale, And Chicken

Preparation Time: 30 minutes
Cooking Time: 30 minutes
Servings: 4
Ingredients:

- 4 cups reduced-sodium chicken broth
- 1 tablespoon extra-virgin olive oil
- 1 small onion, finely chopped
- 1 pound sliced mushrooms
- 1 pound boneless, skinless chicken thighs, cut into bite-size pieces
- 1¼ cups quick-cooking steel-cut oats
- 1 (10-ounce) package frozen chopped kale (about 4 cups)
- ½ cup grated Parmesan cheese (optional)
- Freshly ground black pepper (optional)

Directions:

1. Bring the broth to a simmer over medium-low heat in a medium saucepan.
2. Warm the olive oil in a large, nonstick skillet over medium-high heat. Sauté the onion and mushrooms until the onion is translucent, about 5 minutes. Push the vegetables to the side, and add the chicken. Let it sit untouched until it browns, about 2 minutes.
3. Add the oats. Cook for 1 minute, stirring constantly. Add ½ cup of the hot broth, and stir until it is completely absorbed. Continue stirring in broth, ½ cup at a time, until it is absorbed and the oats and chicken are cooked for about 10 minutes. If you run out of broth, switch to hot water.
4. Stir in the frozen kale, and cook until it's warm. Top with Parmesan and black pepper, if you like.
5. FLAVOR BOOST: Garnish with minced parsley and red pepper flakes. You can substitute ½ cup of dry white wine for ½ cup of chicken broth.
6. INGREDIENT TIP: All varieties of oats have similar amounts of fiber, vitamins, and minerals. The main difference is in how quickly they're digested, with the steel-cut and old-fashioned/rolled oats breaking down more slowly, which is helpful for blood

sugar control. The quick-cooking steel-cut oats used in this risotto are cut into smaller pieces, enabling you to make this dish in under 30 minutes.

Per serving: Calories: 470kcal; Fat:16 g; Carbohydrates: 44g; Protein: 40g

85. Turkey with Leeks and Radishes

Preparation Time: 10 minutes
Cooking Time: 6 hours
Servings: 2
Ingredients:

- 1-pound turkey breast, skinless, boneless, and cubed
- 1 leek, sliced
- 1 cup radishes, sliced
- 1 red onion, chopped
- 1 tablespoon olive oil
- A pinch of salt and black pepper
- 1 cup chicken stock
- ½ teaspoon sweet paprika
- ½ teaspoon coriander, ground
- 1 tablespoon cilantro, chopped

Directions:

1. In your slow cooker, combine the turkey with leek, radishes, onion, and other ingredients. Toss, put the lid on, and cook on High for 6 hours.
2. Divide everything between plates and serve.

Per serving: Calories: 226kcal; Fat: 9g; Carbohydrates: 6g; Protein: 12g

86. Turkey And Cranberry Sauce

Preparation time: 10 minutes
Cooking time: 50 minutes
Servings: 3
Ingredients:

- 1 cup chicken stock
- 2 tablespoons avocado oil
- ½ cup cranberry sauce
- 1 big turkey breast, skinless, boneless, and sliced
- 1 yellow onion, roughly chopped
- Salt and black pepper to the taste

Directions:

1. Heat a pan with the avocado oil over medium-high heat, add the onion and sauté for 5 minutes.
2. Add the turkey and brown for 5 minutes more.
3. Add the rest of the ingredients, toss, introduce in the oven at 350 degrees F and cook for 40 minutes

Per serving: Calories: 382kcal; Fat: 12.6g; Carbohydrates: 26.6g; Protein: 17.6g

87. Coconut Chicken

Preparation time: 10 minutes
Cooking time: 5 minutes
Servings: 3
Ingredients:

- 6 oz chicken fillet
- ¼ cup of sparkling water
- 1 egg
- 3 tablespoons coconut flakes
- 1 tablespoon coconut oil
- 1 teaspoon Greek Seasoning

Directions:

1. Cut the chicken fillet into small pieces (nuggets).

2. Then crack the egg in the bowl and whisk it.
3. Mix up together egg and sparkling water.
4. Add Greek seasoning and stir gently.
5. Dip the chicken nuggets in the egg mixture and then coat in the coconut flakes.
6. Melt the coconut oil in the skillet and heat it until it is shimmering.
7. Then add prepared chicken nuggets.
8. Roast them for 1 minute from each or until they are light brown.
9. Dry the cooked chicken nuggets with the help of a paper towel and transfer them to the serving plates.

Per serving: Calories: 141kcal; Fat: 8.9g; Carbohydrates: 1g; Protein: 13.9g

88. Chicken And White Bean

Preparation Time: 10 minutes
Cooking Time: 70 minutes
Servings: 8
Ingredients:

- 2 tablespoons fresh cilantro, chopped
- 2 cups grated Monterey Jack cheese
- 3 cups water
- 1/8 teaspoon cayenne pepper
- 2 teaspoons pure chile powder
- 2 teaspoon ground cumin
- 1 4-oz can of chopped green chiles
- 1 cup corn kernels
- 2 15-oz cans shite beans, drained and rinsed
- 2 garlic cloves
- 1 medium onion, diced
- 2 tablespoon extra-virgin olive oil
- 1 lb. chicken breasts, boneless and skinless

Directions:

1. Slice chicken breasts into ½-inch cubes, and with pepper and salt, season them.
2. On high fire, place a large nonstick fry pan and heat oil.
3. Sauté chicken pieces for three to four minutes or until lightly browned.
4. Reduce fire to medium and add garlic and onion.
5. Cook for 5 to 6 minutes or until the onions are translucent.
6. Add water, spices, chilies, corn, and beans. Bring to a boil.
7. Once boiling, slow fire to a simmer and continue simmering for an hour, uncovered.
8. To serve, garnish with a sprinkling of cilantro and a tablespoon of cheese.

Per serving: Calories: 433kcal; 21.8Fat: g; Carbohydrates: 29.5g; Protein: 30.6g

89. Ginger Chicken Drumsticks

Preparation time: 10 minutes
Cooking time: 30 minutes
Servings: 4
Ingredients:

- 4 chicken drumsticks
- 1 apple, grated
- 1 tablespoon curry paste
- 4 tablespoons milk
- 1 teaspoon coconut oil
- 1 teaspoon chili flakes
- ½ teaspoon minced ginger

Directions:

1. Mix grated apple, curry paste, milk, chili flakes, and minced garlic.
2. Put coconut oil in the skillet and melt it.
3. Add apple mixture and stir well.

4. Then add chicken drumsticks and mix up well.
5. Roast the chicken for 2 minutes from each side.
6. Then preheat the oven to 360F.
7. Place the skillet with chicken drumsticks in the oven and bake for 25 minutes.

Per serving: Calories: 150kcal; Fat:6.4 g; Carbohydrates: 9.7g; Protein: 13.5g

90. Pomegranate Chicken

Preparation time: 10 minutes
Cooking time: 30 minutes
Servings: 6
Ingredients:

- 1-pound chicken breast, skinless, boneless
- 1 tablespoon za'atar
- ½ teaspoon salt
- 1 tablespoon pomegranate juice
- 1 tablespoon olive oil

Directions:

1. Rub the chicken breast with za'atar seasoning, salt, olive oil, and pomegranate juice.
2. Marinate the chicken for 15 minutes and transfer to the skillet.
3. Roast the chicken for 15 minutes over medium heat.
4. Then flip the chicken to another side and cook for 10 minutes more.
5. Slice the chicken and place it on the serving plates.

Per serving: Calories: 107kcal; Fat: 4.2g; Carbohydrates: 0.2g; Protein: 16.1g

91. Lemon Chicken Mix

Preparation time: 10 minutes
Cooking time: 10 minutes
Servings: 3
Ingredients:

- 8 oz chicken breast, skinless, boneless
- 1 teaspoon Cajun seasoning
- 1 teaspoon balsamic vinegar
- 1 teaspoon olive oil
- 1 teaspoon lemon juice

Directions:

1. Cut the chicken breast into halves and sprinkle with Cajun seasoning.
2. Then sprinkle the poultry with olive oil and lemon juice.
3. Then sprinkle the chicken breast with the balsamic vinegar.
4. Preheat the grill to 385F.
5. Grill the chicken breast halves for 5 minutes from each side.
6. Slice Cajun chicken and place it on the serving plate.

Per serving: Calories: 150kcal; 5.2Fat: g; Carbohydrates: 0.1g; Protein:24.1 g

92. Pork Chops And Relish

Preparation time: 10 minutes
Cooking time: 14 minutes
Servings: 3
Ingredients:

- 6 pork chops, boneless
- 7 ounces marinated artichoke hearts, chopped and their liquid reserved
- A pinch of salt and black pepper
- 1 teaspoon hot pepper sauce
- 1 and ½ cups tomatoes, cubed
- 1 jalapeno pepper, chopped
- ½ cup roasted bell peppers, chopped

- ½ cup black olives, pitted and sliced

Directions:

1. Mix the chops with the pepper sauce and reserved liquid from the artichokes in a bowl, and cover and keep in the fridge for 15 minutes.
2. Heat a grill over medium-high heat, add the pork chops and cook for 7 minutes on each side.
3. In a bowl, combine the artichokes with the peppers and the remaining ingredients, toss, divide on top of the chops and serve.

Per serving: Calories: 215kcal; Fat: 6g; Carbohydrates: 6g; Protein: 35g

93. Lamb And Tomato Sauce

Preparation time: 10 minutes
Cooking time: 55 minutes
Servings: 3
Ingredients:

- 9 oz lamb shanks
- 1 onion, diced
- 1 carrot, diced
- 1 tablespoon olive oil
- 1 teaspoon salt
- 1 teaspoon ground black pepper
- 1 ½ cup chicken stock
- 1 tablespoon tomato paste

Directions:

1. Sprinkle the lamb shanks with salt and ground black pepper.
2. Heat olive oil in the saucepan.
3. Add lamb shanks and roast them for 5 minutes from each side.
4. Transfer meat to the plate.
5. After this, add onion and carrot to the saucepan.
6. Roast the vegetables for 3 minutes.
7. Add tomato paste and mix up well.

8. Then add chicken stock and bring the liquid to a boil.
9. Add lamb shanks, stir well, and close the lid.
10. Cook the meat for 40 minutes over medium-low heat.

Per serving: Calories: 232kcal; Fat: 11.3g; Carbohydrates: 7.3g; Protein: 25.1g

94. Lemony Lamb and Potatoes

Preparation time: 10 minutes
Cooking time: 30 minutes
Servings: 3
Ingredients:

- 2-pound lamb meat, cubed
- 2 tablespoons olive oil
- 2 springs rosemary, chopped
- 2 tablespoons parsley, chopped
- 1 tablespoon lemon rind, grated
- 3 garlic cloves, minced
- 2 tablespoons lemon juice
- 2 pounds of baby potatoes, scrubbed and halved
- 1 cup veggie stock

Directions:

1. In a roasting pan, combine the meat with the oil and the rest of the ingredients, introduce it to the oven and bake at 400 degrees F for 2 hours and 10 minutes.
2. Divide the mix between plates and serve.

Per serving: Calories: 302kcal; Fat: 15.2g; Carbohydrates: 23.3g; Protein: 15.2g

95. Cumin Lamb Mix

Preparation time: 10 minutes
Cooking time: 30 minutes
Servings: 3
Ingredients:

- 2 lamb chops (3.5 oz each)
- 1 tablespoon olive oil
- 1 teaspoon ground cumin
- ½ teaspoon salt

Directions:

1. Rub the lamb chops with ground cumin and salt.
2. Then sprinkle them with olive oil.
3. Let the meat marinate for 10 minutes.
4. After this, preheat the skillet well.
5. Place the lamb chops in the skillet and roast them for 10 minutes. Flip the meat on another side from time to time to avoid burning.

Per serving: Calories: 384kcal; Fat: 33.2g; Carbohydrates: 0.5g; Protein: 19.2g

96. Pork And Figs Mix

Preparation time: 10 minutes
Cooking time: 30 minutes
Servings: 3
Ingredients:

- 3 tablespoons avocado oil
- 1 and ½ pounds pork stew meat, roughly cubed
- Salt and black pepper to the taste
- 1 cup red onions, chopped
- 1 cup figs, dried and chopped
- 1 tablespoon ginger, grated
- 1 tablespoon garlic, minced
- 1 cup canned tomatoes, crushed
- 2 tablespoons parsley, chopped

Directions:

1. Heat your pot with the oil over medium-high heat, add the meat, and brown for 5 minutes.
2. Add the onions and sauté for 5 minutes more.
3. Add the rest of the ingredients, and bring to a simmer. Let it cook over medium heat for 30 minutes more.
4. Divide the mix between plates and serve.

Per serving: Calories: 309kcal; Fat:16 g; Carbohydrates: 21.1g; Protein: 34.2g

97. Greek Styled Lamb Chops

Preparation time: 10 minutes
Cooking time: 4 minutes
Servings: 3
Ingredients:

- ¼ tsp black pepper
- ½ tsp salt
- 1 tbsp bottled minced garlic
- 1 tbsp dried oregano
- 2 tbsp lemon juice
- 8 pcs of lamb loin chops, around 4 oz
- Cooking spray

Directions:

1. Preheat broiler.
2. In a big bowl or dish, combine the black pepper, salt, minced garlic, lemon juice, and oregano. Then rub it equally on all sides of the lamb chops.
3. Then coat a broiler pan with the cooking spray before placing the lamb chops on the pan and broiling until the desired doneness is reached or for four minutes.

Per serving: Calories: 131.9kcal; Fat: 5.9g; Carbohydrates: 2.6g; Protein: 17.1g

98. Pork And Peas

Preparation time: 10 minutes
Cooking time: 30 minutes
Servings: 3
Ingredients:

- 4 ounces of snow peas
- 2 tablespoons avocado oil
- 1 pound pork loin, boneless and cubed
- ¾ cup beef stock
- ½ cup red onion, chopped
- Salt and white pepper to the taste

Directions:

1. Heat your pan with the oil over medium-high heat, add the pork and brown for 5 minutes.
2. Add the peas and the rest of the ingredients, toss, bring to a simmer and cook over medium heat for 15 minutes.
3. Divide the mix between plates and serve right away.

Per serving: Calories: 332kcal; Fat: 16.5g; Carbohydrates: 20.7g; Protein: 26.5g

99. Pork And Sage Couscous

Preparation time: 10 minutes
Cooking time: 8 Hours
Servings: 3
Ingredients:

- 2 pounds pork loin boneless and sliced
- ¾ cup veggie stock
- 2 tablespoons olive oil
- ½ tablespoon chili powder
- 2 teaspoon sage, dried
- ½ tablespoon garlic powder
- Salt and black pepper to the taste
- 2 cups couscous, cooked

Directions:

1. In your slow cooker, combine the pork with the stock, the oil, and the other ingredients except for the couscous. Put the lid on and cook on Low for 7 hours.
2. Divide the mix between plates, add the couscous on the side, sprinkle the sage on top and serve.

Per serving: Calories: 272kcal; Fat: 14.5g; Carbohydrates:16.3 g; Protein: 14.3g

100. Pork Fajitas

Preparation time: 10 minutes
Cooking time: 20 minutes
Servings: 4
Ingredients:

- 1 green bell pepper, julienned
- 1 medium onion, julienned
- 2 garlic cloves, minced
- 1 lb. lean, boneless pork cut into strips
- 1 tsp dried oregano
- 1/2 tsp cumin
- 2 tbsp pineapple juice
- 2 tbsp vinegar
- 1/4 tsp hot pepper sauce
- 1 tbsp canola oil
- 4 flour tortillas, 8" size

Directions:

1. Start by mixing the oregano, garlic, vinegar, cumin, hot sauce, and pineapple juice in a bowl.
2. Place the pork in this marinade and mix well to coat them, then refrigerate for 15 minutes.
3. Meanwhile, preheat your oven to 325 degrees F.
4. Wrap the tortillas in foil and heat them in the oven for 2-3 minutes.
5. Now, heat a suitable grill on medium heat and add pork strips, green peppers, oil, and onion.

6. Cook for 5 minutes until the pork is done.
7. Serve warm in warmed tortillas.

Per serving: Calories: 406kcal; Fat: 18g; Carbohydrates: 34g; Protein:26g

CHAPTER 8: Fish Recipes

101. Salmon with Vegetables

Preparation Time: 10 minutes
Cooking Time: 15 minutes
Servings: 4
Ingredients:

- 2 tablespoons olive oil
- 2 carrots
- 1 head fennel
- 2 squashes
- ¼ onion
- 1-inch ginger
- 1 cup white wine
- 2 cups water
- 2 parsley sprigs
- 2 tarragon sprigs
- 6 oz. salmon fillets
- 1 cup cherry tomatoes
- 1 scallion

Directions:

1. In your skillet, heat olive oil, add fennel, squash, onion, ginger, and carrot, and cook until vegetables are soft
2. Add wine, water, and parsley and cook for another 4-5 minutes
3. Season salmon fillets and place in the pan
4. Cook for 5 minutes per side or until it is ready
5. Transfer salmon to a bowl, spoon tomatoes and scallion around salmon and serve

Per serving: Calories: 301kcal; Fat: 17g; Carbohydrates: 2g; Protein: 8g

102. Crispy Fish

Preparation Time: 5 minutes
Cooking Time: 15 minutes
Servings: 4
Ingredients:

- 4 thick fish fillets
- ¼ cup all-purpose flour
- 1 egg
- 1 cup bread crumbs
- 2 tablespoons vegetables
- Lemon wedge

Directions:

1. In a dish, add flour, egg, and breadcrumbs to different dishes and set aside
2. Dip each fish fillet into the flour, egg, and then bread crumbs bowl
3. Place each fish fillet in a heated skillet and cook for 4-5 minutes per side
4. When ready, remove from pan and serve with lemon wedges

Per serving: Calories: 189kcal; Fat: 17g; Carbohydrates: 2g; Protein: 7g

103. Moules Marinieres

Preparation Time: 10 minutes
Cooking Time: 30 minutes
Servings: 4
Ingredients:

- 2 tablespoons ghee
- 1 leek
- 1 shallot
- 2 cloves garlic
- 2 bay leaves
- 1 cup white win

- 2 lb. mussels
- 2 tablespoons mayonnaise
- 1 tablespoon lemon zest
- 2 tablespoons parsley
- 1 sourdough bread

Directions:

1. In a saucepan, melt ghee, add leeks, garlic, bay leaves, and shallot and cook until vegetables are soft.
2. Bring to a boil, add mussels, and cook for 1-2 minutes.
3. Transfer mussels to a bowl and cover.
4. Whisk in the remaining ghee with mayonnaise and return the mussels to the pot.
5. Add lemon juice and parsley lemon zest and stir to combine.

Per serving: Calories: 321kcal; Fat: 17g; Carbohydrates: 2g; Protein: 9g

104. Steamed Mussels with Coconut-Curry

Preparation Time: 15 minutes
Cooking Time: 20 minutes
Servings: 4
Ingredients:

- 6 sprigs cilantro
- 2 cloves garlic
- 2 shallots
- ¼ teaspoon coriander seeds
- ¼ teaspoon red chili flakes
- 1 teaspoon zest
- 1 can of coconut milk
- 1 tablespoon vegetable oil
- 1 tablespoon curry paste
- 1 tablespoon brown sugar
- 1 tablespoon fish sauce
- 2 lb. mussels

Directions:

1. Combine lime zest, cilantro stems, shallot, garlic, coriander seed, chili, and salt in a bowl.
2. In a saucepan, heat oil. Add garlic, shallots, pounded paste, and curry paste.
3. Cook for 3-4 minutes. Add coconut milk, sugar, and fish sauce.
4. Bring to a simmer and add mussels.
5. Stir in lime juice and cilantro leaves and cook for a few more minutes.
6. When ready, remove from heat and serve.

Per serving: Calories: 209kcal; Fat: 7g; Carbohydrates: 6g; Protein: 17g

105. Tuna Noodle Casserole

Preparation Time: 15 minutes
Cooking Time: 20 minutes
Servings: 4
Ingredients:

- 2 oz. egg noodles
- 4 oz. fraiche
- 1 egg
- 1 teaspoon cornstarch
- 1 tablespoon juice from 1 lemon
- 1 can tuna
- 1 cup peas
- ¼ cup parsley

Directions:

1. Place noodles in a saucepan with water and bring to a boil.
2. Mix egg, crème fraiche, and lemon juice in a bowl, and whisk well.
3. When noodles are cooked, add the crème fraiche mixture to the skillet and mix well.
4. Add tuna, peas, parsley lemon juice, and mix well.

5. When ready, remove from heat and serve.

Per serving: Calories: 214kcal; Fat: 7g; Carbohydrates: 2g; Protein: 19g

106. Salmon Burgers

Preparation Time: 10 minutes
Cooking Time: 15 minutes
Servings: 4
Ingredients:

- 1 lb. salmon fillets
- 1 onion
- ¼ dill fronds
- 1 tablespoon honey
- 1 tablespoon horseradish
- 1 tablespoon mustard
- 1 tablespoon olive oil
- 2 toasted split rolls
- 1 avocado

Directions:

1. Place salmon fillets in a blender and blend until smooth. Transfer to a bowl, add onion, dill, honey, and horseradish, and mix well.
2. Add salt and pepper and form 4 patties.
3. In a bowl, combine mustard, honey, mayonnaise, and dill.
4. In a skillet, heat oil, add salmon patties, and cook for 2-3 minutes per side.
5. When ready, remove from heat.
6. Divided lettuce and onion between the buns.
7. Place salmon patty on top and spoon mustard mixture and avocado slices.
8. Serve when ready.

Per serving: Calories: 189kcal; Fat: 7g; Carbohydrates: 6g; Protein: 12g

107. Seared Scallops

Preparation Time: 15 minutes
Cooking Time: 20 minutes
Servings: 4
Ingredients:

- 1 lb. sea scallops
- 1 tablespoon canola oil

Directions:

1. Season scallops and refrigerate for a couple of minutes.
2. In a skillet, heat oil, add scallops, and cook for 1-2 minutes per side
3. When ready, remove from heat and serve

Per serving: Calories: 283kcal; Fat: 8g; Carbohydrates: 10g; Protein: 9g

108. Black COD

Preparation Time: 15 minutes
Cooking Time: 20 minutes
Servings: 4
Ingredients:

- ¼ cup miso paste
- ¼ cup sake
- 1 tablespoon mirin
- 1 teaspoon soy sauce
- 1 tablespoon olive oil
- 4 black cod filets

Directions:

1. Combine miso, soy sauce, oil, and sake in a bowl.
2. Rub mixture over cod fillets and let it marinade for 20-30 minutes.
3. Adjust broiler and broil cod filets for 10-12 minutes.
4. When fish is cooked, remove and serve.

Per serving: Calories: 213kcal; Fat: 15g; Carbohydrates: 2g; Protein: 8g

109. Miso-Glazed Salmon

Preparation Time: 10 minutes
Cooking Time: 40 minutes
Servings: 4
Ingredients:

- ¼ cup red miso
- ¼ cup sake
- 1 tablespoon soy sauce
- 1 tablespoon vegetable oil
- 4 salmon fillets

Directions:

1. In a bowl, combine sake, oil, soy sauce, and miso.
2. Rub mixture over salmon fillets and marinade for 20-30 minutes.
3. Preheat a broiler.
4. Broil salmon for 5-10 minutes.
5. When ready, remove and serve.

Per serving: Calories: 198kcal; Fat: 10g; Carbohydrates: 5g; Protein: 6g

110. Salmon Pasta

Preparation Time: 10 minutes
Cooking Time: 25 minutes
Servings: 2
Ingredients:

- 5 tablespoons ghee
- ¼ onion
- 1 tablespoon all-purpose flour
- 1 teaspoon garlic powder
- 2 cups skim milk
- ¼ cup Romano cheese
- 1 cup green peas
- ¼ cup canned mushrooms
- 8 oz. salmon
- 1 package of penne pasta

Directions:

1. Bring your pot with water to a boil.
2. Add pasta and cook for 10-12 minutes.
3. In a skillet, melt ghee, add onion and sauté until tender.
4. Stir in garlic powder, flour, milk, and cheese.
5. Add mushrooms and peas and cook on low heat for 4-5 minutes.
6. Toss in salmon and cook for another 2-3 minutes.
7. When ready, serve with cooked pasta.

Per serving: Calories: 211kcal; Fat: 18g; Carbohydrates:7 g; Protein: 17g

111. Crusty Pesto Salmon

Preparation Time: 5 minutes
Cooking Time: 15 minutes
Servings: 2
Ingredients:

- ¼ cup unsalted pistachios, shelled and finely chopped
- ¼ cup pesto
- 2 x 4-oz. salmon fillets
- 2 tbsp. ghee, melted

Directions:

1. Mix the pistachios and pesto.
2. Place the salmon fillets in a round baking dish, roughly six inches in diameter.
3. Brush the fillets with ghee, followed by the pesto mixture, which coats the top and bottom. Put the baking dish inside the fryer.
4. Cook for twelve minutes at 390°F.
5. The salmon is ready when it flakes easily when prodded with a fork. Serve warm.

Per serving: Calories: 290kcal; Fat: 11g; Carbohydrates:5.2 g; Protein: 20g

112. Sesame Tuna Steak

Preparation Time: 5 minutes
Cooking Time: 12 minutes
Servings: 2
Ingredients:

- 1 tbsp. coconut oil, melted
- 2 x 6-oz. tuna steaks
- ½ tsp. garlic powder
- 2 tsp. black sesame seeds
- 2 tsp. white sesame seeds

Directions:
1. Apply the coconut oil to the tuna steaks with a brunch, then season with garlic powder.
2. Combine the black and white sesame seeds. Embed them in the tuna steaks, covering the fish all over. Place the tuna into your air fryer.
3. Cook for eight minutes at 400°F, turning the fish halfway through.
4. The tuna steaks are ready when they have reached a temperature of 145°F. Serve straightaway.

Per serving: Calories: 160kcal; Fat: 6g; Carbohydrates: 3.5g; Protein:26 g

113. Foil Packet Salmon

Preparation Time: 5 minutes
Cooking Time: 15 minutes
Servings: 2
Ingredients:

- 2 x 4-oz. skinless salmon fillets
- 2 tbsp. ghee, melted
- ½ tsp. garlic powder
- 1 medium lemon
- ½ tsp. dried dill

Directions:
1. Cut a sheet of aluminum foil into two squares measuring roughly 5" x 5". Lay each of the salmon fillets at the center of each piece. Brush both fillets with a tablespoon of bullet and season with a quarter teaspoon of garlic powder.
2. Halve the lemon and grate the skin of one half over the fish. Cut four half-slices of lemon, using two to top each fillet. Season each fillet with a quarter teaspoon of dill.
3. Fold the tops and sides of the aluminum foil over the fish to create a kind of packet. Place each one in the fryer.
4. Cook for twelve minutes at 400°F.
5. The salmon is ready when it flakes easily. Serve hot.

Per serving: Calories: 240kcal; Fat: 13g; Carbohydrates: 4g; Protein: 21g

114. Foil Packet Lobster Tail

Preparation Time: 5 minutes
Cooking Time: 15 minutes
Servings: 2
Ingredients:

- 2 x 6-oz. lobster tail halves
- 2 tbsp. salted ghee, melted
- ½ medium lemon, juiced
- ½ tsp. Old Bay seasoning
- 1 tsp. dried parsley

Directions:
1. Lay each lobster on a sheet of aluminum foil. Pour a drizzle of melted ghee and lemon juice over each one, and season with Old Bay.
2. Fold down the sides and ends of the foil to seal the lobster. Place each one in the fryer.
3. Cook at 375°F for twelve minutes.
4. Just before serving, top the lobster with dried parsley.

Per serving: Calories: 510kcal; 18Fat: g; Carbohydrates: 9g; Protein: 26g

115. Creamy Tuna, Spinach, and Eggs Plates

Preparation time: 5 minutes.
Cooking time: 0 minutes.
Servings: 2
Ingredients:

- 2 ounces spinach leaves
- 2 ounces tuna, packed in water
- 2 eggs, boiled
- 4 tablespoon cream cheese, full-fat
- Seasoning:
- ¼ teaspoon salt
- 1/8 teaspoon ground black pepper

Directions:

1. Take two plates and evenly distribute spinach and tuna between them.
2. Peel the eggs cut them in half, divide them between the plates, and then season with salt and black pepper.
3. Serve with cream cheese.

Per serving: Calories: 212kcal; Fat: 14.1g; Carbohydrates: 3.5g; Protein: 18g

116. Baked Fish with Feta and Tomato

Preparation time: 5 minutes
Cooking time: 15 minutes
Servings: 2
Ingredients:

- 2 pacific whitening fillets
- 1 scallion, chopped
- 1 Roma tomato, chopped
- 1 teaspoon fresh oregano
- 1-ounce feta cheese, crumbled

Seasoning:

- 2 tablespoon avocado oil
- 1/3 teaspoon salt
- 1/4 teaspoon ground black pepper
- ¼ crushed red pepper

Directions:

1. Turn on the oven, set it to 400°F, and let it preheat.
2. Take a medium skillet pan, place it over medium heat, add oil and when hot, add scallion and cook for 3 minutes.
3. Add tomatoes, stir in ½ teaspoon oregano, 1/8 teaspoon salt, black pepper, and red pepper, pour in ¼ cup water, and bring it to simmer.
4. Sprinkle the remaining salt over fillets, add to the pan, drizzle with the remaining oil, and then bake for 10 to 12 minutes until fillets are fork-tender.
5. When done, top the fish with the remaining oregano and cheese and serve.

Per serving: Calories: 427.5kcal; Fat: 29.5g; Carbohydrates: 8g; Protein: 26.7g

117. Cod and Mushrooms Mix

Preparation Time: 10 minutes
Cooking Time: 25 minutes
Servings: 4
Ingredients:

- 2 cod fillets, boneless
- 4 tablespoons olive oil
- 4 ounces mushrooms, sliced
- Sea salt and black pepper to the taste
- 12 cherry tomatoes, halved
- 8 ounces lettuce leaves, torn
- 1 avocado, pitted, peeled, and cubed
- 1 red chili pepper, chopped
- 1 tablespoon cilantro, chopped
- 2 tablespoons balsamic vinegar
- 1-ounce feta cheese, crumbled

Directions:

1. Put the fish in a roasting pan, brush it with 2 tablespoons oil, sprinkle salt and pepper all over and broil under medium-high heat for 15 minutes. Meanwhile, heat your pan with the rest of the oil over medium heat, add the mushrooms, stir and sauté for 5 minutes.
2. Add the rest of the ingredients, toss, cook for 5 minutes more, and divide between plates.
3. Top with the fish and serve right away.

Per serving: Calories:257 kcal; Fat: 10g; Carbohydrates: 24.3g; Protein: 19.4g

118. Salmon Panatela

Preparation Time: 5 minutes
Cooking Time: 22 minutes
Servings: 4
Ingredients:

- 1 lb. skinned salmon, cut into 4 steaks each
- 1 cucumber, peeled, seeded, cubed
- Salt and black pepper to taste
- 8 black olives, pitted and chopped
- 1 tbsp capers, rinsed
- 2 large tomatoes, diced
- 3 tbsp red wine vinegar
- ¼ cup thinly sliced red onion
- 3 tbsp olive oil
- 2 slices zero carb bread, cubed
- ¼ cup thinly sliced basil leaves

Directions:

1. Preheat a grill to 350°F and prepare the salad. Mix the cucumbers, olives, pepper, capers, tomatoes, wine vinegar, onion, olive oil, bread, and basil leaves in a bowl. Let sit for the flavors to incorporate.

2. Season the salmon steaks with salt and pepper; grill them on both sides for 8 minutes. Serve the salmon steaks warm on a bed of veggies salad.

Per serving: Calories:338 kcal; Fat: 27g; Carbohydrates: 1g; Protein: 25g

119. Blackened Fish Tacos with Slaw

Preparation Time: 5 minutes
Cooking Time: 20 minutes
Servings: 4
Ingredients:

- 1 tbsp olive oil
- 1 tsp chili powder
- 2 tilapia fillets
- 1 tsp paprika
- 4 low carb tortillas
- Slaw: ½ cup red cabbage, shredded
- 1 tbsp lemon juice
- 1 tsp apple cider vinegar
- 1 tbsp olive oil
- Salt and black pepper to taste

Directions:

1. Season the tilapia with chili powder and paprika.
2. Heat the olive oil in a skillet over medium heat.
3. Add tilapia and fry until blackened, about 3 minutes per side.
4. Cut into strips. Divide the fish among the tortillas.
5. To serve, combine all slaw ingredients in a dish and top with the fish.

Per serving: Calories: 268kcal; Fat: 20g; Carbohydrates:5 g; Protein: 18g

120. Red Cabbage Tilapia Taco Bowl

Preparation Time: 5 minutes
Cooking Time: 20 minutes
Servings: 4
Ingredients:

- 2 cups caulis rice
- 2 tsp ghee
- 4 tilapia fillets, cut into cubes
- ¼ tsp taco seasoning
- Salt and chili pepper to taste
- ¼ head red cabbage, shredded
- 1 ripe avocado, pitted and chopped

Directions:

1. Sprinkle caulis rice in a bowl with a bit of water and microwave for 3 minutes. Fluff after with a fork and set aside. Melt ghee in a skillet over medium heat, rub the tilapia with the taco seasoning, salt, and chili pepper, and fry until brown on all sides, for about 8 minutes.

2. Transfer to a plate and set aside. In 4 serving bowls, share the caulis rice, cabbage, fish, and avocado. Serve with chipotle lime sour cream dressing.

Per serving: Calories:269 kcal; Fat: 24g; Carbohydrates: 4g; Protein: 15g

CHAPTER 9: 30-Day Meal Plan

Days	Breakfast	Lunch	Dinner	Snack
1	Easy Asparagus Quiche	Wild Rice Prawn Salad	Miso-Glazed Salmon	Blueberry Cauliflower
2	Summer Veggie Omelet	Grilled Chicken	Cinnamon Roll Oats	Basil & Walnut Pesto
3	Mexican Style Burritos	Tuna Noodle Casserole	Banana Quinoa	Roasted Red Endive With Caper Butter
4	Turkey And Spinach Scramble On Melba Toast	Black Cod	Turkey And Cranberry Sauce	Cinnamon Maple Sweet Potato Bites
5	Cheesy Scrambled Eggs With Fresh Herbs	Spinach Wrap	Salmon With Vegetables	Strawberry Frozen Yogurt
6	Smoothie With Ginger And Cucumber	Pomegranate Chicken	Garlic Mushroom Chicken	Potato Chips
7	White Bean Smoothie	Seared Scallops	Cherry Berry Bulgur Bowl	Raw Broccoli Poppers
8	Lean And Green Chicken Pesto Pasta	Orzo And Veggie Bowls	Cumin Lamb Mix	Wheat Crackers
9	Mexican Scrambled Eggs In Tortilla	Couscous With Artichokes, Sun-Dried Tomatoes And Feta	Salmon Burgers	Rosemary & Garlic Kale Chips
10	Egg And Veggie Muffins	Pork And Sage Couscous	Fennel Wild Rice Risotto	Roasted Radishes
11	Green Tea Purifying Smoothie	Foil Packet Salmon	Vanilla Oats	Collard Greens And Tomatoes
12	Apple Pumpkin Muffins	Crispy Fish	Lamb And Tomato Sauce	Radish Hash Browns
13	Zucchini Egg Casserole	Peanut Butter And Cacao Breakfast Quinoa	Salmon Panatela	Asparagus Frittata

14	Oatmeal Blast With Fruit	Turkey With Leeks And Radishes	Coconut Chicken	Mozzarella Cauliflower Bars
15	Clean Liver Green Juice	Red Cabbage Tilapia Taco Bowl	Bell Peppers 'N Tomato-Chickpea Rice	Grape, Celery & Parsley Reviver
16	Spiced French Toast	Pork Chops And Relish	Chicken With Potatoes, Olives & Sprouts	Walnut & Spiced Apple Tonic
17	Breakfast Smoothie	Buckwheat And Grapefruit Porridge	Creamy Tuna, Spinach, And Eggs Plates	Honey Chili Nuts
18	Sweet Pancakes	Oat Risotto With Mushrooms, Kale, And Chicken	Lemon Chicken Mix	Candied Ginger
19	Breakfast Tacos	Baked Fish With Feta And Tomato	Crunchy Quinoa Meal	Chia Crackers
20	Vegetable Omelet	Mint Quinoa	Pork And Figs Mix	Roasted Asparagus
21	Cheesy Scrambled Eggs With Fresh Herbs	Baked Curried Apple Oatmeal Cups	Cod And Mushrooms Mix	Strawberry Frozen Yogurt
22	Smoothie With Ginger And Cucumber	Ginger Chicken Drumsticks	Foil Packet Lobster Tail	Potato Chips
23	White Bean Smoothie	Blackened Fish Tacos With Slaw	Raspberry Overnight Porridge	Raw Broccoli Poppers
24	Lean And Green Chicken Pesto Pasta	Salmon Pasta	Chicken And White Bean	Wheat Crackers
25	Summer Veggie Omelet	Brown Rice Pilaf With Butternut Squash	Steamed Mussels With Coconut-Curry	Roasted Radishes
26	Mexican Style Burritos	Lemony Lamb And Potatoes	Apple Oatmeal	Collard Greens And Tomatoes
27	Turkey And Spinach Scramble On Melba Toast	Moules Marinieres	Seeds And Lentils Oats	Radish Hash Browns

28	Zucchini Egg Casserole	Pork And Peas	Greek Styled Lamb Chops	Blueberry Cauliflower
29	Oatmeal Blast With Fruit	Quinoa And Potato Bowl	Sesame Tuna Steak	Basil & Walnut Pesto
30	Clean Liver Green Juice	Pork Fajitas	Crusty Pesto Salmon	Roasted Red Endive With Caper Butter

Conversion Chart

Volume Equivalents (Liquid)

US Standard	US Standard (ounces)	Metric (approximate)
2 tablespoons	1 fl. oz.	30 mL
¼ cup	2 fl. oz.	60 mL
½ cup	4 fl. oz.	120 mL
1 cup	8 fl. oz.	240 mL
1½ cups	12 fl. oz.	355 mL
2 cups or 1 pint	16 fl. oz.	475 mL
4 cups or 1 quart	32 fl. oz.	1 L
gallon	128 fl. oz.	4 L

Volume Equivalents (Dry)

US Standard	Metric (approximate)
⅛ teaspoon	0.5 mL
¼ teaspoon	1 mL
½ teaspoon	2 mL
¾ teaspoon	4 mL
1 teaspoon	5 mL
1 tablespoon	15 mL
¼ cup	59 mL
⅓ cup	79 mL
½ cup	118 mL
⅔ cup	156 mL

¾ cup	177 mL
1 cup	235 mL
2 cups or 1 pint	475 mL
3 cups	700 mL
4 cups or 1 quart	1 L

Oven Temperatures

Fahrenheit (F)	Celsius (C) (approximate)
250°F	120°C
300°F	150°C
325°F	165°C
350°F	180°C
375°F	190°C
400°F	200°C
425°F	220°C
450°F	230°C

Weight Equivalents

US Standard	Metric (approximate)
½ ounce	1g
1 ounce	3g
2 ounces	6g
4 ounces	11g
8 ounces	22g

12 ounces	34g
16 ounces or 1 pound	45g

Index

Roasted Asparagus; 37
Roasted Radishes; 37
Roasted Red Endive With Caper Butter; 40
Roasted Vegetable Salad; 41
Rosemary & Garlic Kale Chips; 36
Salmon & Arugula Salad; 43
Salmon Burgers; 69
Salmon Panatela; 73
Salmon Pasta; 70
Salmon with Vegetables; 67
Seafood Arugula Salad; 47
Seared Scallops; 69
Seeds And Lentils Oats; 53
Sesame Tuna Steak; 71
Smoked Salad; 47
Smoothie With Ginger And Cucumber; 32
Spanish Tomato Salad; 42
Spiced French Toast; 26
Spinach Wrap; 54

Springtime Chicken Berries Salad; 46
Steamed Mussels with Coconut-Curry; 68
Strawberry Frozen Yogurt; 38
Summer Veggie Omelet; 28
Sweet Pancakes; 28
Toasted Mango Pepitas Kale Salad; 45
Toaster Almond Spiralized Beet Salad; 46
Tuna Noodle Casserole; 68
Turkey And Cranberry Sauce; 60
Turkey and Spinach Scramble on Melba Toast; 30
Turkey with Leeks and Radishes; 60
Vanilla Oats; 56
Vegetable Omelet; 31
Walnut & Spiced Apple Tonic; 38
Watercress Salad; 47
Wheat Crackers; 35
White Bean Smoothie; 33
Wild Rice Prawn Salad; 49
Zucchini Egg Casserole; 29

Conclusion

Liver disease is not a death sentence; it may be treated to the point that you can enjoy all parts of your life. The first signs of a failing liver include foul breath, bloating, heartburn, sudden weight loss, and premature graying of the hair. Countless fatty liver sufferers show no symptoms or adverse effects until too late. You need to be more vigilant and adjust your diet and lifestyle. The recipes in this cookbook can help you avoid developing a fatty liver. In general, we should examine how the liver and the rest of the body are affected by fatty liver. Proactiveness is essential. If you wait until the last minute, you may miss out on opportunities. Be mindful of your liver's capacity. The best way to start is to take it one step at a time. Follow the recipes in this book, and you'll be on your way to a healthy liver. I hope your health continues to improve in the years to come. As a result of this procedure, you will feel rejuvenated.

Of course, not everyone will be receptive to the method. Still, none of the ingredients used are dangerous, and the results speak for themselves.

39569765R00046